Introduction

Background of the City

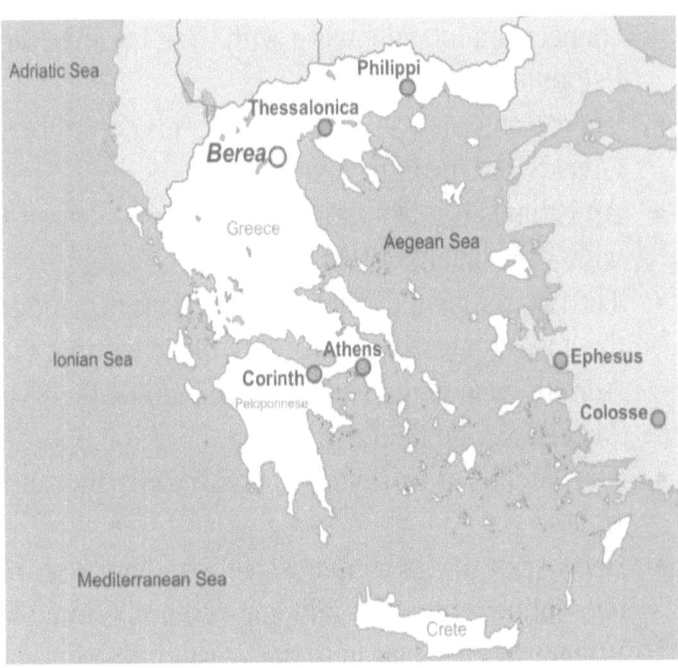

- Understanding the city of Corinth during the time of writing is a vital component to understanding what Paul

had to say to the church
- Corinth was a major city before it was destroyed in around 146 BC
- The city of Corinth laid in ruins for 100 years until it was rebuilt by Julius Caesar in 44 BC
- The city quickly rose back to its place of prominence
- Corinth was a prominent city-state and capital in the Greek province of Achaia (pronounced: Ah-Ky-Yuh)
- Corinth was the fourth largest city of the Roman Empire (behind Rome, Athens and Alexandria)
- The city of Corinth would have had a population of about 80,000 in Paul's day (an additional 20,000 would have resided in surrounding cities and villages)
- Corinth is located on a narrow strip of land that connects mainland Greece with what is called the Peloponnese to the south
- We call this area an isthmus. Isthmus comes from the Greek word meaning "neck"
- An isthmus is a land bridge, or a narrow strip of land with a sea on either side
- The two ports on either side of Corinth became two of the busiest ports in the world (Gulf of Corinth via the Adriatic Sea on the West and the Saronic Gulf via the Aegean Sea on the East)
- The isthmus of Corinth is approximately four miles wide
- Because of the geographical setting, there were really two options for doing shipping and trade from the Eastern Mediterranean to the Western Mediterranean or vice versa
- First, would be to sail all the way around the peninsula
- Sailing around to the south of the Peloponnese

peninsula was extremely dangerous
- The first century Roman geographer Strabo, said, "if sailors pass the southern tip twice, they ought to forget their homes."
- In other words, you may get lucky once, but it is unlikely that you would twice
- It was also very time consuming. It was around 200 extra miles of sailing to go around
- They tried unsuccessfully to build a canal there to make travel safer and quicker
- A canal does exist there currently, but it wasn't completed until 1893
- The second option for shipping, trade and travel was to unload and manually carry cargo across the four-mile isthmus and re-load on the other side
- They had actually built a road across the isthmus which had grooves in in. They would have trolleys of some sort to transport cargo or even small boats from one side to the other and offload onto another ship (See picture below)
- All the trade from the Eastern Mediterranean to the Western Mediterranean was funneled through the city of Corinth
- This made Corinth a very important place
- Where the crews waited in line for their cargo to be moved across the isthmus, they spent a lot of time. And where people spend time, they spend money
- This made Corinth a busy and prosperous city
- Also because of the presence of trade and ships, the city was very transient
- Because people did not often stay long, it very much contributed to the immorality

- The presence of travelers created a great opportunity for people to hear the gospel and take it back with them to their homes
- Corinth was known to be very racially diverse
- Corinth was also known to be very religiously diverse and free
- Corinth was known as a destination for religious pilgrims including Jews
- We saw in the book of Acts that Aquila and Priscilla ended up there after the Jews were expelled from Rome by Emperor Claudius
- It is estimated that 2/3 of the population of the city was slave
- It is estimated that there were 26 different temples or shrines dedicated to various gods in Corinth
- There was a major Temple to Apollo located there
- There was a temple to Asklepion there where people would go for healing
- One of the most prominent religions of Corinth was the worship of Aphrodite (Latin: Venus), the goddess of love
- The Temple to Aphrodite was located in what is called the Acrocorinth or Upper Corinth which stood 1,886 feet above the city
- There were said to be 1,000 female slaves dedicated to the worship of Aphrodite at her temple
- There were many other pagan temples throughout the city
- We know that there was a Jewish population in Corinth
- We know that when Paul went to Corinth in Acts 18, there was a synagogue there

- - Acts 18:4 - [4] Every Sabbath he reasoned in the synagogue, trying to persuade Jews and Greeks
- Corinth was well known for its immorality
- The term "Corinthian" became slang for all immorality and loose living
- Corinth had gained a reputation for immorality and perversity that Greek writer Aristophanes (450-385 B.C.) created the Greek verb *korinthiazo* which means to act like a Corinthian specifically referring to fornication and sexual immorality
- It was said that to "behave as a Corinthian was to live immorally"
- The term "Corinthian girl" became a term used to refer to prostitutes wherever they were located
- It was classified as the most sinful city in the world
- The immoral nature of the city contributed to Paul's concern for the church. There is no doubt that the church at Corinth was impacted by living in a place like Corinth
- Every two years Corinth hosted the Isthmian games which was an Olympic type games. On a couple of occasions Paul uses metaphors that may have been connected to these games
- Corinth was well-known for having what the Romans called "patrons". This was a term used to refer to wealthy families who took on other people as their clients. These patrons provided support, money, jobs and various other things in return for services and even political support.
- Not only would the church have been impacted by the

immorality of the world in which they lived, they also
had to battle Greek thinking which opposed the Truth
- Corinth, although a part of the Roman Empire was also
a Greek influenced (Hellenistic) city
- We can see the impact of Greek philosophy on the
church. Specifically, we see the church having been
influenced by Greek dualism (Plato) and Gnosticism
- Churches today still are products of the world in which
they live and sometimes have to be un-taught and
specifically trained to think counter culturally

The Background to the Church At Corinth

- Paul first came to the city of Corinth during his second
missionary journey in about 52 AD where the church
was established
- The book of Acts provides an account of Paul's work in
Corinth
    - **Acts 18:1-16** - After this, Paul left
Athens and went to Corinth. [2] There he met a
Jew named Aquila, a native of Pontus, who
had recently come from Italy with his wife
Priscilla, because Claudius had ordered all
Jews to leave Rome. Paul went to see
them, [3] and because he was a tentmaker as
they were, he stayed and worked with
them. [4] Every Sabbath he reasoned in the
synagogue, trying to persuade Jews and
Greeks. [5] When Silas and Timothy came from
Macedonia, Paul devoted himself exclusively
to preaching, testifying to the Jews that Jesus
was the Messiah. [6] But when they opposed

Paul and became abusive, he shook out his clothes in protest and said to them, "Your blood be on your own heads! I am innocent of it. From now on I will go to the Gentiles."

[7] Then Paul left the synagogue and went next door to the house of Titius Justus, a worshiper of God. [8] Crispus, the synagogue leader, and his entire household believed in the Lord; and many of the Corinthians who heard Paul believed and were baptized. [9] One night the Lord spoke to Paul in a vision: "Do not be afraid; keep on speaking, do not be silent. [10] For I am with you, and no one is going to attack and harm you, because I have many people in this city." [11] So Paul stayed in Corinth for a year and a half, teaching them the word of God. [12] While Gallio was proconsul of Achaia, the Jews of Corinth made a united attack on Paul and brought him to the place of judgment. [13] "This man," they charged, "is persuading the people to worship God in ways contrary to the law." [14] Just as Paul was about to speak, Gallio said to them, "If you Jews were making a complaint about some misdemeanor or serious crime, it would be reasonable for me to listen to you. [15] But since it involves questions about words and names and your own law—settle the matter yourselves. I will not be a judge of such things." [16] So he drove them off. [17] Then the crowd there turned on Sosthenes the

> synagogue leader and beat him in front of the proconsul; and Gallio showed no concern whatever.

- Paul spent a year and a half in Corinth during his initial visit
- It was there that he probably wrote 1 and 2 Thessalonians
- Paul spent three months in Corinth during his third visit (second extended stay)
- It was from Corinth that Paul wrote the book of Romans during his second extended stay
- It was in Corinth that Paul became acquainted with Priscilla and Aquila
- We have reason to believe that there was contact with the church at Corinth after Paul's time there and before the writing of 1 Corinthians
- There was evidently a member of the church by the name of Chloe who had (or someone in her household) reported to Paul some of the inner turmoil in the church
    - **1 Corinthians 1:11** - [11] My brothers and sisters, some from Chloe's household have informed me that there are quarrels among you.
- The Corinthian church had also evidently written Paul for some answers to some questions that they had
    - **1 Corinthians 7:1** - Now for the matters you wrote about: "It is good for a man not to have sexual relations with a woman."
- Some think there may have even been a letter written by Paul to the church at Corinth before 1 Corinthians was penned

- - **1 Corinthians 5:9** - [9] I wrote to you in my letter not to associate with sexually immoral people—
- Some people even think that there was letter written by Paul to Corinth after 1 Corinthians and before 2 Corinthians
  - - **2 Corinthians 2:4** - [4] For out of much affliction and anguish of heart I wrote to you with many tears; not so that you would be made sorrowful, but that you might know the love which I have especially for you.
    - **2 Corinthians 7:8** - [8] For though I caused you sorrow by my letter, I do not regret it; though I did regret it—*for* I see that that letter caused you sorrow, though only for a while
- Some would even suggest that 2 Corinthians 10-13 is actually this sorrowful letter
- However, it seems likely that there were at least three letters written by Paul to Corinth and three separate visits
- We think it is likely that Paul made multiple trips to the city of Corinth
  - - We know that there were two trips and likely a third
    - **2 Corinthians 13:2** - [2] I already gave you a warning when I was with you the second time. I now repeat it while absent: On my return I will not spare those who sinned earlier or any of the others
- It seems like the letter deals with both issues brought to Paul's attention by someone else (1 Corinthians 1-6)

and the theological questions that the church asked of
Paul (1 Corinthians 7-16)
* It is likely that although Paul had some Jewish converts,
the majority of the church was Gentile and maybe even
slave.

Author: Paul

* There is not generally a ton of debate about Paul's
authorship
* Twice in this letter Paul cites himself as the author
  ○ **2 Corinthians 1:1** - Paul, an apostle of Christ
  Jesus by the will of God,
  and Timothy *our* brother, To the church of
  God which is at Corinth with all the saints
  who are throughout Achaia:
  ○ **2 Corinthians 10:1** - Now I, Paul,
  myself urge you by the meekness and
  gentleness of Christ—I who am meek when
  face to face with you, but bold toward you
  when absent!
* Several of the early church fathers referenced this letter
and attributed it to Paul (Polycarp, Irenaeus, Clement of
Alexandria, Tertullian, Cyprian)

Date: 57 AD

* It is likely that Paul wrote 1 Corinthians in early 57 AD
* A few months after writing, Paul left Ephesus and
headed towards Corinth by way of Macedonia
* It was from Macedonia that Paul wrote 2 Corinthians in
wake of Titus' report
* We will give it a date of 57 AD, or about 6 months after

the writing of 1 Corinthians

Quick overview of Paul's dealings with the Church at Corinth

- Paul established the church on his second missionary journey (52 AD)
- He may have written a letter to Corinth dealing with some issues which is now lost
- The Corinthians probably followed up that letter with a letter to Paul asking some questions
- Sometime in between this and 1 Corinthians being written, Paul received a report from Chloe's household about the condition of the church
- Paul sent Timothy to Corinth
- Paul wrote 1 Corinthians from Ephesus (About 57 AD)
- Then he likely made a second, unplanned, quick trip to Corinth in what he called a "painful visit" (2 Corinthians 2:1, 13:2)
- Some suggest that there was a "sorrowful letter" that was written that has also been lost
- Titus was sent to Corinth in wake of this
- It seems Titus straightened some of this out and reported this to Paul. This prompted Paul to write 2 Corinthians
- It was following this that Paul made another trip to Corinth where he stayed for 3 months and wrote the book of Romans
- Following this he most likely left for Jerusalem, perhaps with the offering

Purpose: Paul's defense of his apostleship

- 2 Corinthians contains the most systematic defense that

Paul will give of his authority as an apostle

- He will confront clear opponents to his apostleship
- It seems that some people in the church had arisen who claimed to be apostles, but were not
- He will also give clear proofs of his apostleship
- We will also notice a focus on the concept of suffering

Key Word: Glory

- The word glory appears 21 times in this letter
- The concept of glory seems to be a prominent theme in this chapter

Style:

- We will notice that 2 Corinthians does not use the same style as 1 Corinthians
- 1 Corinthians was an organized letter, which seemed to in an orderly way deal with questions that were given to Paul
- 2 Corinthians is very theological, but also seems to be slightly less orderly
- 2 Corinthians is more theological than 1 Corinthians
- The letter has an encouraging tone for the first 9 chapters
- Chapters 10-13 are much more harsh in their tone
- 2 Corinthians also is a place where we gain a lot of personal information from Paul

2 Corinthians 1

1:1

- This is a very typical greeting for Paul as well as a typical first century formula for introducing a letter
- First century letters often began with naming the sender, rather than only a signature at the end of the letter
- It is typical for Paul to state the fact that he is an apostle
- Paul is emphasizing his authority
- Notice also that he is an apostle "by the will of God"
- His position is an apostle is not something he was voted into or campaigned for
- The defense of his own apostleship is a key throughout 2 Corinthians
- Once again Paul has to establish the legitimacy of his apostleship because his call to that office was different from the others
- Here, he also mentions Timothy as being along with him
- Timothy is also mentioned as a co-sender in several other New Testament letters (1 & 2 Thessalonians, Philippians, Colossians and Philemon)
- Timothy had been dispatched to Corinth at some point in time just prior to the sending of 1 Corinthians
- It is likely that Timothy was not well received there and that his stay was cut short
- He also establishes here that this letter was specifically intended for the church at Corinth
- It was also secondarily for those in the broader region of Achaia
- The region of Achaia was sometimes used to refer to the southern part of Greece, however, here it likely is just pointing to the surrounding area

1:2

- Paul also uses the traditional greeting of grace and peace
- It was not uncommon for a letter to begin with some sort of

general well wishing
- Grace was the Gentile way of greeting
- Peace was the Jewish way of greeting
- Paul is asking God to bestow grace to them in that they needed the grace of God to sustain themselves
- He is asking for God to grant them peace in that they may live in harmony with one another and with the community
- When the Jews would say "*shalom*" it was a wish for the benefit of the whole person
- The source of that grace and peace was clearly stated to be "God our Father and our Lord Jesus Christ"
- There is something to be said about the mentioning of Jesus alongside God the Father

1:3

- Paul will dive into this letter with a doxology
- Often times in Paul's letters he begins with some form of thanksgiving
    - **Romans 1:8** - [8] First, I thank my God through Jesus Christ for you all, because your faith is being proclaimed throughout the whole world
    - **1 Corinthians 1:4** - [4] I thank my God always concerning you for the grace of God which was given you in Christ Jesus
    - **Ephesians 1:3** - [3] Blessed *be* the God and Father of our Lord Jesus Christ, who has blessed us with every spiritual blessing in the heavenly *places* in Christ
    - **Colossians 1:3** - [3] We give thanks to God, the Father of our Lord Jesus Christ, praying always for you
    - **1 Thessalonians 1:2** - [2] We give thanks to God always for all of you, making mention *of you* in our prayers
    - **2 Thessalonians 1:3** - [3] We ought always to give thanks to God for you, brethren, as is *only* fitting, because your faith is greatly enlarged, and the love of each one of you toward one another

> grows *ever* greater

- This also may have sounded similar to a typical blessing pronounced inside a Jewish Synagogue except for the fact that God is called "the Father of Jesus"
- Now, God is not just the Father of Abraham, Isaac and Jacob, He is the Father of our Lord Jesus Christ
- He calls for God to be "blessed" or "praised"
- He refers to God in two different ways as he introduces this doxology
- Both of these speak about God being the God over some type of blessing which He dispenses to His people
- First, he is the Father of mercies
- The "father of" means that he is the giver of mercies
- The mercies which Paul speaks of most likely points to his tender compassion and kindness towards mankind
- Second, He is the God of all comfort
- The word "comfort" is the Greek word *paraklésis* (παράκλησις) and means "come to the aide"
- This word for "comfort" will appear 29 times in the book of 2 Corinthians
- The word "comfort" will appear 10 times in this section (both as a noun and a verb)
- There are other times similar language is used
  - He is the God of love and peace (2 Corinthians 13:11)
  - He is the God of hope (Romans 15:13)
  - He is the God of peace (Romans 16:20)
  - He is the God of perseverance and encouragement (Romans 15:5)

1:4

- Here he mentions the activity of the God of all comfort as well as the reasoning for the giving of the comfort
- First, he mentions that the God of all comfort comforts us in all our afflictions
- The word "affliction" is the Greek word *thlipsis* (θλῖψις) which

means pressure, distress, or tribulation
- We do not know what afflictions Paul has in mind here
- This may point to general afflictions that every Christian may face
- I certainly believe that the principle rings true in general for every person
- This may point to specific apostolic sufferings
- This may point to specific events in his own life
- Perhaps it speaks of some of the good news that Paul received about the Corinthian church by way of Titus
- Perhaps it speaks of deliverance from some of the oppositions he faced especially in Ephesus
- Throughout 2 Corinthians Paul spoke about his hardships, persecutions, dangers, opposition, and pressures (2 Corinthians 4:7-12, 11:23-29)
- Comfort in the midst of affliction may not always mean that one is delivered from the thing doing the afflicting
- Paul spoke later about the affliction of a "thorn in his flesh" which God did not and would not remove
- The comfort we receive in our suffering may simply be the courage to remain faithful in spite of the affliction
- The comfort we receive in our suffering may be the removal of the anxiety we face and the peace that passes all understanding
- The Bible certainly teaches on numerous occasions that the Christian life is sometimes marked by suffering and affliction
- Even in the midst of our affliction, we can be reminded that God is the God of all comfort and He is the Father of mercies
- We can find comfort from God in the midst of affliction
- Second, he states that God provides that comfort so that they can in turn give comfort to others who are afflicted
- This may be both a purpose and a result of God's comfort to us
- Meaning God may provide comfort to people for the purpose of them turning around and using their experience to help others going through similar situations
- I believe that when we have gone through a trial or affliction, we are able to better empathize and relate to those going through similar things

- We have a responsibility to use that and help others
- It also may just be a natural result of being comforted in affliction
- It is difficult for the one who is underneath a heavy load to give someone else a hand
- This makes clear that the comfort may not be deliverance because a person may not be able to provide that type of comfort to someone else
- Suffering and affliction has made me a better minister
- God comforts us so that we might be comforters ourselves
- We do not always have answers to give to the afflicted
- We can't always make sense of suffering for someone else
- We do not always have a way out for them in their affliction
- However, we do have an example to show and a hand of help to extend
- We can help bear someone else's burdens
- We can weep with those who weep
- We can provide love and prayers
- We can provide encouragement to remain faithful
- We can provide a testimony of faithfulness ourselves

1:5

- Paul speaks here of Christ's sufferings abounding
- The word for abound here means to overflow
- The sufferings of Christ might point back to the physical suffering that Jesus endured in his beatings and crucifixion
- As he connects Christ's sufferings to his own sufferings, there are two things in mind
- First, Paul connects himself to Christ's actual suffering
- Paul certainly does connect himself to Christ's sufferings other places
  - **2 Corinthians 4:10** - [10] We always carry around in our body the death of Jesus, so that the life of Jesus may also be revealed in our body.
  - **Philippians 3:10** – [10] I want to know Christ—yes, to know the power of his resurrection and participation

in his sufferings, becoming like him in his death

- A person shares in Christ's sufferings when they suffer for the cause of Christ
- Secondly, this speaks of how the sufferings of Christ are the sufferings that His followers undergo as they themselves are associated with Christ
- He is suggesting that the suffering that he faces is part of being a follower of Christ sometimes
- Jesus made it clear that this would be a mark of the apostles' own lives
- This all may apply in general to the suffering of life, but Paul has in mind the suffering that Christians face on account of Christ
- Paul seems to view his own suffering as a continuation of Jesus' suffering
- In fact, Paul's sufferings are counted as being Christ's sufferings
- The Lord asked Saul, "why do you persecute me?"
- Paul claims that this suffering was his in abundance
- Where suffering comes in abundance, comfort comes in abundance also
- The more we share in Christ's own sufferings in this way, the more comfort we receive
- We cannot out suffer the comfort of God
- One of the ways that God bestows comfort is through other people who have been comforted
- We can also receive comfort from Jesus because He suffered and was faithful
- Jesus can comfort us because he himself was acquainted with suffering (Isaiah 53:3)
- Remember, "He comforts us so that we might comfort others with the comfort we ourselves have received"
- Jesus was strengthened by an angel after his temptation
    - **Matthew 4:11** - [11] Then the devil left him, and angels came and attended him.
- Jesus was strengthened by an angel at Gethsemane in the midst of His agony
    - **Luke 22:43** - [43] An angel from heaven appeared to

him and strengthened him.
- He is a perfect example of faithfulness in the midst of suffering and He is able to minister to us because of that
    - **Hebrews 4:15** - [15] For we do not have a high priest who is unable to empathize with our weaknesses, but we have one who has been tempted in every way, just as we are—yet he did not sin.
    - **Hebrews 12:3** - [3] Consider him who endured such opposition from sinners, so that you will not grow weary and lose heart.
    - **1 Peter 2:21** - [21] To this you were called, because Christ suffered for you, leaving you an example, that you should follow in his steps.

1:6

- In this verse, Paul will speak of the benefit of both his suffering and comfort to the Corinthians
- Paul states first that the suffering that he has undergone was for the Corinthians own spiritual benefit
- He says that his own suffering benefited them in two ways spiritually
- First, it was for their own comfort
- Paul's affliction produces comfort for the Corinthians in that it leaves an example for them of how to remain faithful in trials
- Second, it was for their own salvation
- Some have suggested that some in Corinth may have seen the suffering and affliction which Paul faced as a strike against him
- We might wonder how does Paul's own personal affliction have bearing on the salvation of anyone else
- Paul's suffering was not redemptive suffering like Jesus' was
- Paul is stating that he suffered en route to bringing the Gospel to them
- Paul's afflictions came as a result of the Gospel, which has the power to save
- Paul certainly had affliction, but it was a part of bringing the gospel to them

- In other words, it was various afflictions and oppositions that may have charted his course towards Corinth, which resulted in their hearing and obeying the Gospel
- Also, Paul's faithfulness in the face of affliction allowed them to hear and obey the Gospel. If he had backed down, they would not have been blessed in that way
- Next, he speaks of the benefit of the comfort that he received
- He repeats the idea that the comfort he received would benefit the Corinthians in themselves being comforted when they suffered affliction
- When he says that the comfort is effective in patient endurance, he means that the comfort that is received produces their patient endurance
- When we receive comfort in the midst of suffering, it helps us to have patient endurance through them
- Notice that it does not assure deliverance from the affliction, but only comfort which helps one to endure
- The presence of "patient endurance" indicates the rescue may not be on the horizon
- This endurance is not just being strong willed or more determined, it involves an abiding trust in God's goodness and faithfulness in the wake of affliction

1:7

- When Paul speaks of his "steadfast hope for you" he means his hope for the Corinthian Christians to patiently endure afflictions
- The word for "steadfast" is the Greek word *bebaios* (βέβαιο) which means "firm, enduring, sure or solid footing
- Even though throughout 1 Corinthians and even 2 Corinthians, the church seemed to be shaky at best, Paul is confident that they will stay faithful in the face of affliction
- Paul then describes the Corinthians as sharers in both their sufferings and their comfort
- We do not know what suffering the Corinthians had undergone, but apparently in some way they understood the idea of affliction

- The word "sharers" is the same word often translated "fellowship" and is means to share something in common
- They are sharers not only of Paul's suffering, but of Christ's suffering as spoken of in verse 5
- The Apostles did not have the market on affliction cornered. The church at Corinth evidently had people who were suffering greatly

1:8

- This verse makes it absolutely clear that sometimes God allows people to face more than they can handle in themselves
- People will sometimes quote 1 Corinthians 10:13 out of context to suggest that God never gives more than we can handle
- Paul says that he faced more than he could handle in himself
- Paul will on numerous occasions in this epistle recount his suffering for the cause of the Gospel
- Specifically here he points to affliction he faced while in Asia
- The term Asia is a reference to the area we know of today as modern day Turkey
- We are not exactly sure what afflictions Paul has in mind
- Perhaps he points to his time in Ephesus and the riot that was begun by Demetrious (Acts 19:23-41)
- Perhaps it speaks of the "fighting wild beasts" in Ephesus (1 Corinthians 15:32)
- Some think maybe it speaks to the occasion that Priscila and Aquila "risked their necks" for him
    - **Romans 16:4** - ⁴They risked their lives for me. Not only I but all the churches of the Gentiles are grateful to them.
- Or maybe it just points to a series of difficulties and oppositions throughout his missionary journeys
- Acts records other sufferings that Paul faced including an imprisonment in Philippi
- One would not have to look hard to see times of great affliction in the life of Paul
- The affliction he faced cause Paul to despair of life

- The word despair is the word *exaporeó* (ἐξαπορέομαι) means at a dead end or on a road with no exit
- Sometimes our afflictions feel like they will never end
- Yet later Paul says that our present sufferings are "light and momentary" (4:17)
- The load that Paul was carrying was more than he could carry on his own
- Perhaps these afflictions not only threatened his physical life, but caused him to long for Heaven

1:9

- When Paul says "we had the sentence of death ourselves" it is speaking of a feeling he had in himself about the end result of his affliction
- Paul felt that the situation he was in would result in death
- Paul's suffering was beyond his ability to endure it without help, but it was not beyond God's ability
- In fact, it seems that this gives some sort of purpose to God allowing these afflictions
- This was so that they may not trust in themselves, but that they may trust more deeply in God
- The point is that often we cannot remedy outside situations, but God can provide comfort and deliverance
- Sometimes we only come to trust God over ourselves through affliction
- While affliction may be something that we would want to avoid, it also offers a great lesson for its students
- The Corinthians may have been tempted to trust on their own wisdom, knowledge and abilities in the midst of their own affliction
- The lesson for anyone in the midst of suffering is that we should place unwavering trust in God
- This language may be similar to Abraham's sentiments towards his son, Isaac, whom he felt had a sentence of death. However, Abraham believed that God could raise the dead
  - **Hebrews 11:19** - [19] Abraham reasoned that God

could even raise the dead, and so in a manner of speaking he did receive Isaac back from death.

- God is able to overturn the sentence of death that Paul felt and bring life from it
- I do not believe that Paul is saying that he expected if he was killed that he would be resurrected
- His focus seems to be on the fact that if God can raise the dead back to life that He is also able to remove the feeling of impending death and even deliver from affliction
- If God can raise the dead, He can handle whatever afflictions we may face
- Our belief in a God who can raise the dead back to life is foundational to our faith
- Paul taught in Romans that the Abrahamic type of faith which saves is a faith of life from death
    - **Romans 4:17** - [17] As it is written: "I have made you a father of many nations." He is our father in the sight of God, in whom he believed—the God who gives life to the dead and calls into being things that were not.
- Our faith in a God who can even raise the dead back to life is essential to us and will dictate how we handle afflictions in our own life
- A God who can give life to dead things can handle whatever situations we face in this life

1:10

- Paul says that he was delivered from whatever affliction he faced in Asia without the result of death which he expected
- It literally says that he was delivered from "such a great" death
- Perhaps the idea is that it was "such a great death" because it was such a terrible situation that could have ended so terribly for Paul
- Notice that it was not fate that delivered him, it was God who delivered him
- He also speaks of his expectation of future deliverance

- Perhaps here he has in mind specific opposition that he is facing
- Three times in this verse it speaks of God's deliverance
- The first time it was in the past tense
- The second and third time the deliverance speaks of something in the future
- It could be that Paul is saying, "God did deliver in the past, he will deliver me in the future from this current opposition and I trust that He will continue to deliver me as well"
- While God does not always deliver us from every affliction that we face, we should have a confidence that He is able to
- When Paul speaks of future deliverance, he speaks of his "hope"
- This hope was not a wishful thinking, but a confident expectation
- Paul's view of future deliverance was based on two things
- First, it was based on his view of God's power and ability
- In the previous verse he spoke about believing in a God who can raise the dead
- Second, it was based on his past experience
- When God has delivered you in the past, it gives more reason to be confident that He can in the future
- God has a track record of delivering His people
- Paul had experienced this deliverance from affliction on other occasions
    - **2 Timothy 4:17-18** - ¹⁷ But the Lord stood with me and strengthened me, so that through me the proclamation might be fully accomplished, and that all the Gentiles might hear; and I was rescued out of the lion's mouth. ¹⁸ The Lord will rescue me from every evil deed, and will bring me safely to His heavenly kingdom; to Him *be* the glory forever and ever. Amen.
- Perhaps Paul saw that even death would be form rescue or deliverance from affliction

1:11

- He begins this verse by speaking to their actions and help in his deliverance

- Paul fully believed that it was God who would provide deliverance from afflictions; however, he did not discount the idea that the prayers of God's people contributed to that
- The word translated "joining in helping us" is the Greek word *sunupourgeó* (συνυπουργέω) means to closely cooperate with or to help together
- The idea is that the Corinthians, by praying have joined together with them and God to bring about deliverance
- Paul is saying that the Corinthians helped in a sense
- Our prayers of supplication are not just token acts, they are actually a help to others
- The Corinthians did not cause his deliverance from affliction, but their prayers were answered
- We may be reminded of Peter's deliverance from prison coinciding with the church having a prayer meeting
    - **Acts 12:5** - [5] So Peter was kept in the prison, but prayer for him was being made fervently by the church to God.
- The prayers of the church did not bring about the deliverance, but to say that they did not contribute to God's action would be false
- It also seems that here Paul suggests that in prayer, there is power in numbers
- It literally reads, "thanks may be given by many faces because many faces prayed"
- This picture is of those many faces looking up to heaven
- If many people are praying and God answers those many prayers, the result will be many people thanking God for answered prayer
- The end result of all of this was not Paul's deliverance, but it was many people's thanksgiving

1:12

- In Paul's letters to the Corinthians he speaks often about boasting

- In fact, 29 times in the Corinthians letters the word appears
- When Paul speaks of "boasting" in positive light, he is not speaking of ungodly bragging or arrogance
- By boasting here, Paul speaks of his "proud confidence"
- Paul presents this boast so that the Corinthians can better understand him and his ministry
- The conduct of Paul's ministry is something that God is witness to as well
  - **2 Corinthians 2:17** - [17] For we are not like many, peddling the word of God, but as from sincerity, but as from God, we speak in Christ in the sight of God.
  - **2 Corinthians 4:2** - [2] but we have renounced the things hidden because of shame, not walking in craftiness or adulterating the word of God, but by the manifestation of truth commending ourselves to every man's conscience in the sight of God.
- His confidence or boasting comes because of his clear conscience
- The thing Paul wants to boast of is the testimony of his conscience
- When he refers to his conscience testifying he is saying that his conscience could be called as a witness in his defense
- The only one who could challenge the testimony of his conscience would be God
- Paul is saying that he has examined himself and his actions and he feels no reason for guilt when it comes to his moral conduct
- Just because Paul's conscience is clear does not assure that he has done right
- However, the testimony of his conscience was displayed through his daily, outward actions
- Paul is saying that he has lived a life of integrity
- His integrity was on display in the world and among the church
- Paul defines his character in the world and among the Corinthians in three ways
- First he says it was marked with holiness
- Due to a slight textual variant some versions say "simplicity"

here instead of holiness
- Second, he says that his character was marked by godly sincerity
- This means that his motives were pure
- Third, he says that is was not with fleshly wisdom
- To further clarify his conduct he says that his life was not lived with "fleshly wisdom"
- Fleshly wisdom would refer to the popular morality of the day
- Paul's conscience was not trained by the fleshly wisdom of the day nor by his own fleshly desires
- His conscience was trained by godly values
- If there was a strain on the relationship between Paul and the Corinthian church it was not because of some defect in Paul's morals or character

1:13-14

- In verse 12, Paul is pointing out that his conduct bears witness to his character
- In verse 13, Paul will point out that his writings bear witness to him as well
- His letters have revealed truth, they have revealed his heart and his intentions
- The letters that serve to defend him are his previous letter, 1 Corinthians, perhaps there was a lost "severe letter" and 2 Corinthians as well
- There is substantial writing from Paul to defend himself
- It seems evident that some were misunderstanding Paul even though it should have been clear
- Admittedly, people have and will continue to distort Paul's writing
    - **2 Peter 3:16** - [16] as also in all *his* letters, speaking in them of these things, in which are some things hard to understand, which the untaught and unstable distort, as *they do* also the rest of the Scriptures, to their own destruction.
- It is likely that his letters and his life were under attack from the Corinthians

- Here, he makes plain that what he has written is true and understandable to them
- His epistles did not give his opponents any legitimate reason to attack him
- Specifically, he may be referencing any area where he wrote that might be used against him by his detractors
- It is probable that not only did he want the Corinthians to understand the content, but also his tone
- Sometimes tone can be lost in the midst of a writing
- When he speaks of the ability to understand his letters, perhaps he is suggesting that some of the misunderstanding is deliberate
- In general, his letters are straight forward
- People did not have to wonder what he meant by the things he said
- They needed professional help to misconstrue his instruction to them

1:15-16

- It seems that one of the issues that the Corinthians had with Paul was his slight changes in travel plans
- It seems strange that they would show so little grace in the change of plans
- In 1 Corinthians 16, Paul told the Corinthians that he would come to them after going through Macedonia
- From what we can gather, Paul made a quick, unplanned trip to Corinth before these plans were carried out as well
- In other words, Paul made a visit before going through Macedonia and it was a very brief visit
- The issue may be that his visit was not according to his plans and that it was just a passing visit
- He had promised them a longer stay
- Paul would carry out his original travel plans, but it would be after the painful visit and after writing 2 Corinthians
- The plans that he made were still being carried out even as he wrote 2 Corinthians. The only difference was an unexpected visit in between

- This is why he speaks of his initial plans to come to them
- When Paul says that they might twice receive a blessing there are several things he could have in mind
- First, he could speak of being blessed on two occasions because of two different visits
- Second, he could speak of being blessed by Paul's visit and being blessed by the opportunity to help Paul
- Third, he could be speaking of two opportunities to help Paul
- The emphasis may be on the help that the Corinthians give more than the help that they themselves receive
- Here he even speaks of helping Paul on his journey
- We also should add to this that Paul speaks of the collection for the poor saints in Jerusalem with the same word "grace" as is used here
- Sometimes the greatest blessing is in what we give more than in what we receive

1:17

- Paul knew some were challenging Paul as being fickle
- They were associating his change of plan with a compromise of character
- In this verse he will ask two questions to defend himself
- First, Paul asks, "was I vacillating?" or "did I do it lightly?"
- The obvious answer is "no"
- The point he is making is that sometimes circumstances prompt changes of plans
- Second, Paul asks, "do I purpose according to the flesh?" or "do I make plans like the rest of the world does?"
- The world may make plans with no intention of follow through
- Paul is saying that when he spoke of his plans, he had every intention of following through with them, but circumstances forced a change
- He says with me there will be a yes, yes and a no, no at the same time
- This sounds like Jesus' teaching about vows and oaths
    - **Matthew 5:37** - ³⁷ But let your statement be, 'Yes,

yes' *or* 'No, no'; anything beyond these is of evil.

- The church would have known that Jesus expected a person's word to carry weight
- The Corinthians were not allowing for any reasonable change of plan, but were questioning his very word and his honesty
- Paul's unexpected visit was not a matter of fickleness or dishonesty…it was just a change of plans due to unexpected circumstances
- The repeating of the words "yes" and "no" are for emphasis
- The doubling of the words makes the word that is doubles more firm
- It would be like saying, "again and again yes" and "again and again no"
- It is to suggest that Paul does not talk out of both sides of his mouth

1:18

- Here, Paul is emphasizing the faithfulness of God
- There is some question whether he is teaching a theological truth here or whether he is stating this as a basis for an oath of sorts
- It certainly seems that Paul is in these last verses of the chapter calling God as his witness
- In the previous verses, he called his conscience, his actions and his writings as witnesses. Now, he calls God as a witness
- Paul's change in plans are not an indictment on the faithfulness of God
- He is asserting that since God is faithful, that his word as an apostle is reliable as well
- Also, Paul's change of plans was according to the will of God
- God could verify that Paul was not giving them misleading information about his travel plans
- The Corinthians were accusing Paul of saying "yes" and "no" at the same time
- However, this is not within Paul's character

1:19

- He uses the example of Jesus as well
- He suggests that Jesus was the one who was preached among them
- This would be an example that they would resonate with
- Paul says that Jesus is not "yes" and "no"
- In other words, Jesus' word is not unreliable
- Jesus did not make promises out of both sides of his mouth
- Hebrews says, "he is the same yesterday, today and forever"

1:20

- This verse helps to expound upon what he meant in verse 19
- Here, the emphasis is on the reliability of His promises
- He says, "for as many as are the promises of God"
- This would remind the reader that God has given many promises to His people
- He also makes it clear that those promises are fulfilled in Christ
- God's general promises of salvation were fulfilled in Christ (i.e. the promise to Abraham)
- God's messianic promises are all fulfilled in Christ
- God's specific promises to individuals are available to those in Christ
- There is something to be said about the promises of God being able to be claimed as one is in Christ
- He says that "through us" the amen is spoken
- There is some question about what exactly this phrase means
- First, we need to know the meaning of the word "amen"
- The word "amen" is a Hebrew word that conveyed agreement with what was being said
- Second, we need to know who the "us" is
- The word us seems to be speaking of Paul as well as those who preached Christ to the Corinthians
- The "yes" is in Christ
- Our "yes" as a response is through Christ
- Paul is saying that his preaching is an agreement that God's promises are fulfilled in Christ
- His preaching and convictions are a way of saying, "I agree that

the promises of God are yes in Christ"

- Furthermore, if they join in that "amen" with Paul, they should not doubt his trustworthiness either

1:21-22

- In verses 21 and 22, Paul will use four different phrases to describe what God has done
- First, he speaks of the fact that God establishes us all
- This word here can mean "confirm, make firm, ratify, guarantee or make reliable"
- This word was used in the legal sense of a guarantee that commitments will be carried out
- This both carries the idea of the assurance of a covenant as well as continuing the idea of the reliability of the word spoken
- Second, he says that he has anointed us
- When we think of anointing, we are reminded that in the Old Testament, prophets, priests and kings were anointed
- In the Old Testament, the idea was of the Holy Spirit coming upon a person to help them with the task the were set apart to do
- The Holy Spirit came upon people to help them to do a job that they could not do on their own
- The idea could be that "he has commissioned us" with a specific function that He is going to help us to carry out
- In this case, it could be for preaching the Gospel
- Here, the idea would be connected to the indwelling gift of the Holy Spirit
- Third, he says that he has set his seal of ownership on us
- Sometimes a seal was to denote ownership of something
- Sometimes a seal was to denote the authenticity of something
- The word "seal" was used for sealing of letters to assure that they are not tampered with
- Sometimes a seal was also to guarantee the quality of something
- Paul told the Corinthians that they were the seal of his own apostleship
  - **1 Corinthians 9:2** - [2] If to others I am not an apostle, at least I am to you; for you are the seal of

my apostleship in the Lord.
- In Ephesians, the indwelling of the Holy Spirit is referred to as a seal
    - **Ephesians 1:13** - In Him, you also, after listening to the message of truth, the gospel of your salvation—having also believed, you were sealed in Him with the Holy Spirit of promise
    - **Ephesians 4:30** - ³⁰ Do not grieve the Holy Spirit of God, by whom you were sealed for the day of redemption.
- The focus in this verse is that the seal of the Holy Spirit residing in a believer denotes His ownership
- We as Christians, have been set apart from the world and we belong to God
- Fourth, he says that He has put His Spirit in our hearts
- A person receives the indwelling gift of the Holy Spirit at their baptism
- Paul says that this gift of the Holy Spirit is a pledge
- The word "pledge" is the Greek word *arrabón* (ἀρραβών) which means earnest money or the first installment payment, or a down payment
- The indwelling gift of the Holy Spirit reminds us that there is more to come that relates to our redemption
- The idea of a pledge also conveys the idea that the one who is given the down payment will uphold their end of the bargain
- Receiving the rest of the promises that God has made to us is conditional upon our covenant loyalty
- The Holy Spirit is a pledge to us that more is to come associated with us being made firm in Christ
- Perhaps this points back to the fact that the promises of God are "yes" in Christ
- We can know that God is faithful to His promises to us because He has given us a down payment

1:23

- Paul does not give the specific reason for his change of travel

plans
- However, he does do a couple of things
- First, he calls upon God as his witness
- The whole conversation that he has had in this first chapter has seemed like a defense attorney calling witnesses to the stand
- Paul is treating this like he is on trial before the Corinthians
- Previously, he called his conscience to the stand as well as his own writing
- God is Paul's witness as to the reasons that he changed his plans of travel
- Specifically, God can testify that Paul's motives were not impure
- Paul had already established that God is faithful and that His Word is dependable
- God is a reliable witness to say the least
- There are other places that Paul calls God as a witness on his behalf
    - **Romans 1:9** - [9] For God, whom I serve in my spirit in the *preaching of the* gospel of His Son, is my witness *as to* how unceasingly I make mention of you,
    - **Philippians 1:8** - [8] For God is my witness, how I long for you all with the affection of Christ Jesus.
    - **1 Thessalonians 2:5** - [5] For we never came with flattering speech, as you know, nor with a pretext for greed—God is witness
    - **2 Corinthians 11:31** - [31] The God and Father of the Lord Jesus, He who is blessed forever, knows that I am not lying.
- Remember, Paul told the Corinthians at the end of 1 Corinthians that he planned to do two things
    1. Travel to them through Macedonia sometime after Pentecost
    2. Stay for an extended time
- However, upon receiving word from Timothy, we believe that Paul made a quick, unplanned visit that did not go well
- Also, Paul would eventually follow those plans, it just so

happens that there was an intermediate visit between the carrying out of those initial plans
- The would not concede that the change of plans was prompted by the circumstances
- They want to know why he didn't stay with them very long like he promised
- They also want to know why he has postponed his next visit with them
- The Corinthians were accusing Paul of either lying or have ulterior motives for the change of plan
- He is letting them know that only God can judge his motives, but his motives are pure
- Calling God as his witness is not just words, this was an oath of sorts. Paul was saying, "if I am lying, God can deal with me"
- Second, he reveals that his change of plans was for them
- He says that his change of plan was to spare them
- We might ask: spare them what?
- It is most likely that due to the way things were going that he means that it was to spare them of his righteous anger and a strong rebuke
- There are other instances where Paul makes it quite plain that when he visits, he will deal very sternly with people at Corinth
  - **1 Corinthians 4:19-21** - [19] But I will come to you soon, if the Lord wills, and I shall find out, not the words of those who are arrogant but their power. [20] For the kingdom of God does not consist in words but in power. [21] What do you desire? Shall I come to you with a rod, or with love and a spirit of gentleness?
  - **2 Corinthians 13:2** - [2] I have previously said when present the second time, and though now absent I say in advance to those who have sinned in the past and to all the rest *as well*, that if I come again I will not spare *anyone*,
- Perhaps Paul left Corinth quickly during that intermediate visit to avoid some type of emotion filled confrontation
- Paul speaks of another possible letter in between 1 and 2

Corinthians, which seems that Paul did not spare their feelings
- We do not know why he chose not to fight that battle at that time in Corinth?
- Perhaps his emotions were too high as this was very personal. It is possible to be right and wrong at the same time. Paul had the right position, but maybe he wanted to make sure he handled it with the right spirit
- Perhaps the timing wasn't right and he knew it
- There is nothing wrong with bold confrontation at times
- Jesus boldly confronted the religious leaders on several occasions

1:24

- Paul had already said that his not coming was in order to spare them, it was an act rooted in love for them
- His not staying longer or postponing his plans was also connected to his authority over them
- Paul had the authority to correct and rebuke them because he was an apostle
- If Paul can spare them, this means he also can rebuke them
- However, Paul was not one to abuse his authority
- His goal was never to come and just blast them or inflict some type or ecclesiastical punishment upon them
- He wanted them to deal with the problems in the church
- He wanted them to correct the issues not just because he commanded it, but because they wanted to do the right thing
- Given the personal nature of some of this conflict, it would be tempting for Paul to say, "do what I say because I am an apostle and I am forcing you…or else."
- Paul's goal was not just to alter the actions, but for inward heart change
- There is a great danger of a leader lording their authority over the ones they lead
    - **1 Peter 5:3** - ³nor yet as lording it over those allotted to your charge, but proving to be examples to the flock

- ○ **Matthew 20:25-26** - [25] But Jesus called them to Himself and said, "You know that the rulers of the Gentiles lord it over them, and *their* great men exercise authority over them. [26] It is not this way among you, but whoever wishes to become great among you shall be your servant
- Paul did not lord it over them because his office was "apostle", not Lord
- He says that they are co-workers with the Corinthians
- Paul never treated anyone like they were subordinate to him
- Paul's goal is not to stand over them, but to work alongside them
- Paul and the Corinthians are serving the same God and working towards the same goal
- Even when Paul brought a stern rebuke, it was for the good of the kingdom and for their joy's sake
- The last statement of this chapter is "for in your faith you are standing firm"
- However, it does not seem this is intended to affirm that they are standing strong in their faith
- It is more likely that he is making a statement that "it is by an ongoing faith that you stand firm"
- He said that "we do not lord it over you". Meaning, they do not lord their apostolic authority over their faith
- However, it is by their own faith that they must stand firm in Christ

2 Corinthians 2

2:1

- Paul has been explaining why he changed his travel plans
- At the end of chapter 1, Paul said that he either did not stay long or postponed his next visit in order to spare the Corinthians
- Now, he states that he did not want to make another sorrowful visit
- This infers two things:
- First, that Paul made a visit to Corinth in between 1 and 2 Corinthians being written
- Second, it infers that the visit was not a pleasant visit
- It is because of the nature of that quick, sorrowful visit that Paul was not keen on the idea of having another visit like it
- It is very evident that the idea of the sorrow that came about by his previous visit was very prominent in his mind
- Seven times in verses 1-5 Paul uses the word "sorrow"
- The word translated "sorrow" is the Greek word *lupe* (λύπη) which can also mean grief or pain
- Paul may have in mind the sorrow or pain that the visit caused to himself
- He also may have in mind the sorrow or pain which his visit inflicted upon others
- In other words, another sorrowful visit would be spiritually counter-productive
- It seems that the result of a visit without some type of change in circumstances would not only produce sorrow

2:2

- Here we find that part of the sorrow was a sorrow that went to the Corinthians
- The sorrow in mind is a sorrow that comes about as a result of their sin
- Paul was saying that he did not want to cause them unnecessary pain

- Perhaps this means that there was sometimes a necessary pain
- Later, we will see that Paul intentionally brought them to a point of sorrow over sin
- Certainly, Paul would be willing to dish out a rebuke that caused sorrow if it was beneficial or necessary
- Sometimes it would be necessary to inflict sorrow that repentance and joy may come about
- If the rebuke just causes sorrow, but not repentance, it would not be accomplishing what it needed to accomplish
- There is a difference between a gentle rebuke and beating someone down
- Perhaps Paul felt that he has already said what needed to be said and anything further would be like kicking someone when they were down
- Further, he is saying that if he adds to their sorrow, then they would not themselves be in a place where they could give him joy
- They could not give him joy because they would not have any joy to give
- Paul is not suggesting that by just ignoring their sin that they would be more happy or joyful
- The expectation is that the Corinthian's sorrow would move them to repentance
- It is their sincere repentance which would produce joy

2:3

- When Paul speaks of "the thing I wrote to you" we think it speaks of harsh letter sent after 1 Corinthians
- Some argue that this refers to 1 Corinthians itself, but I think the evidence points away from this
- This gives us the reason for the writing of this letter
- The reason was so that he would not have sorrow when he made his visit
- The thing that would have brought Paul sorrow was to see the church in such bad spiritual condition or being led astray by false teachers

- He had hoped a letter would lead to repentance
- We do not know the contents of this letter, but we can determine some of it based off of things said about in 2 Corinthians

- We are quite certain that it contained instructions for how the church should deal with those who had been openly opposing him in Corinth Also, this appropriate response of repentance would cause Paul himself joy
- Paul ends this verse by speaking of the confidence he has that his joy would be the joy of them all
- He is saying that he was confident that they would positively respond to his rebuke and that their repentance would bring both he and the church a measure of joy

2:4

- Paul makes clear that while he did in fact write a very stern letter that may have caused much sorrow to the readers that his intention was not to hurt them
- Paul was never seeking to cause emotional pain to his readers
- That does not mean that he avoiding speaking the truth, it just means that his goal was never to hurt the Corinthians
- He says that he wrote that letter out of much "affliction and anguish of heart"
- He also says that he wrote it with many tears
- He did not write this with an attitude of payback or doing harm
- He did not write this letter carelessly or flippantly
- He did not receive some type of personal joy by writing such a strong letter
- Paul did not get some type of enjoyment out of giving a needed rebuke
- He says that the reason he wrote to them was so that they might know the love that he has for them
- Sometimes this type of love prompts a strong correction
- Sometimes discipline is difficult for the person giving the discipline
- This letter was not an emotional response rooted in anger

- Whenever we give spiritual correction to a person we need to make sure that it is rooted in love and that the best interest of the offender is in mind

2:5

- Paul will reference here the specific actions of one person in the church
- Paul does not give specific details, but only speaks in generalities
- He does not reveal the person's name nor does he reveal the nature of the offense
- He merely refers to this person by saying "if any has caused sorrow"
- There are a few things that are clear though about this situation
- One thing that is clear is that the issue is one that the Corinthians were well aware of it
- Secondly, it is also clear that the thing in mind was a big part of the issue which prompted the sorrowful letter
- Thirdly, the person's sin had deeply hurt Paul and also caused grief for the church as a whole
- Fourthly, the offender had repented of his sin
- Many have tried to identify the offender as the person mentioned in 1 Corinthians 5
- It is quite possible that this is the exact person in mind, however, it could also be reference to some other situation
- The principles of the restoration of a repentant person certainly do apply here
- This seems to be speaking to someone that had in some way sinned against Paul himself
- Notice that Paul says that the offender had caused Paul some level of personal sorrow
- However, he points out that he has caused the church even more sorrow
- He has caused the church sorrow because perhaps some had been misled by him
- He has caused the church sorrow because his actions affected

Paul's interactions with the church
- He has caused the church sorrow because the church lost God's blessing because of his sin
- He has caused the church sorrow because the church had to discipline this man
- He has caused the church sorrow because this man's actions hurt the church's reputation

2:6

- It is the instruction here that makes one think that the immoral brother of 1 Corinthians 5 is the person in mind here
- Whatever the case it seems that the person spoken of here was one who the whole church exacted some type of church discipline
- We do not know the exact punishment that the majority enforced upon him
- Perhaps it spoke of some type or removal from the church and disfellowshipping
- Whatever the case is, Paul deemed that it was sufficient
- There is such a thing as being too harsh with a person
- He means that the length of time that this person has been removed from the fellowship was long enough to accomplish the intended goal
- The goal of the discipline in 1 Corinthians 5 was that the body of sin would be done away with. In other words, the removal from the church was to cause the man to repent
- The church discipline was not intended to be punitive, but it was to be corrective
- The punishment would no longer be necessary if the intended result was accomplished

2:7

- When Paul says, "on the contrary" he means as opposed to continuing to enforce whatever church discipline they exacted
- They are instructed to do two things

- First, they are told that they should forgive him
- The wound was personal to Paul and also to the church
- There would have been people who were hurt and sinned against by this man (whoever he was)
- The idea that he urges forgiveness implies that the man is repentant
- Jesus taught the same idea of forgiving those who wronged us when they repent
    - **Luke 17:3-4** - [3] Be on your guard! If your brother sins, rebuke him; and if he repents, forgive him. [4] And if he sins against you seven times a day, and returns to you seven times, saying, 'I repent,' forgive him."
- If the repentant man was not forgiven, it would be the church that was now guilty of wrongdoing
- If this is referencing the immoral brother, remember, the church was reluctant to discipline this man. Paul; had to write to them to tell them to do it. Notice, Paul does not gloat and say, "see, I told you this would work."
- The forgiveness would include individuals personally offering forgiveness
- The forgiveness would also include a restoration of his relationship with the church
- Just because forgiveness and restoration occurs does not mean that he would not have some lingering consequences
- If a person was stealing money from the church, they can be forgiven and restored, but that does not mean that they are made the church treasurer
- Second, they are told to comfort him
- It is not enough for this man to be forgiven and restored to fellowship
- This man might be genuinely broken over his sin
- As a result, he does not need to be kicked while he is down, he needs to be comforted
- The comfort would not mean that the man would be told that his sin was inconsequential
- The comfort would have to be in the assurance of his

forgiveness from God and man
- Then, Paul gives the reason for giving this man forgiveness and comfort
- The reason is so that he is not overwhelmed by excessive sorrow
- The word "overwhelmed" is the Greek word *katapino* (καταπίνω) which means drowned or overwhelmed
- It was fine that the man had godly sorrow that led him to repentance
- The danger would be that excessive sorrow would cause him to drown in personal guilt
- It is implied that if a person is overwhelmed with sorrow that they may leave the faith altogether
- Churches run the risk of running to one extreme or the other. One extreme is being too lax. The other extreme is being too harsh
- It is wrong to ignore discipline and correction from sin. It is equally as wrong to continue punishing after repentance has taken place

2:8

- Paul will give a further and more pointed instruction for how the church should deal with this man who was now repentant
- He tells the church that they need to reaffirm their love for him
- The word "reaffirm" is the Greek word *kuroo* (κυρόω) which means to make valid or authoritative or ratify
- The word was used in Galatians 3 to speak of the ratifying of a covenant
    - **Galatians 3:15** - [15] Brethren, I speak in terms of human relations: even though it is *only* a man's covenant, yet when it has been **ratified**, no one sets it aside or adds conditions to it.
- Paul is calling for more than just words, he is calling upon them to act in such a way towards this man that makes it clear that they forgive him and restore him to fellowship
- It seems that the action that Paul was calling for was some type of public action meant to take place in the assembly

- It is the idea of removing any of the punishments that the church levied against him as a means of church discipline
- This would mean that he was welcome back into the church family with no barriers to real fellowship
- There is a time for disfellowship, but there is also a time for re-instatement

2:9

- Paul gives us another reason that he wrote a letter rather than making another visit
- Once again, the letter he is speaking of is the sorrowful letter, not 2 Corinthians
- He says that it was to test to see whether the church was obedient in all things
- He had evidently given them some type of instruction that it was expected that they obeyed
- The word "test" is the Greek word *dokimé* (δοκιμή) means trial, proof, or proven character
- The word was used for the testing of metals to prove their genuineness
- The primary way that they can prove their real character is through obedience
- The obedience was not just to Paul, the obedience was ultimately obedience to Christ
- The church's willingness to accept correction and to repent of their wrongdoing would show a lot about the genuineness of their character
- It seems that Paul is implying that the Corinthians had passed this test and proven that their character is genuine

2:10

- Paul speaks further here about the forgiveness that the congregation should offer to the offender
- Notice that Paul does not say anything about God's forgiveness
- We have to believe that God was willing to forgive this man for

whatever sin he committed based off of his genuine repentance
* If the immoral brother of 1 Corinthians 5 is in mind, we have to wonder what the connection is between the church community and this man's sin
* The sin of incest was not a sin against the church, but the chaos, division and harming of witness was something that was against the church as a whole
* It also seems that Paul is allowing for them to make a personal judgment here
* Paul's forgiveness was not actually contingent upon the church's forgiveness of this man
* Paul is saying that if they make a decision as an autonomous body, Paul will support it
* It is clear that Paul has already personally dealt with this
* He says, "what I have forgiven…"
* It is interesting that he says that he offered this forgiveness "for your sake"
* In what way was Paul's forgiveness of this person for the sake of the Corinthians
* Perhaps it was so that he could lead by example
* Perhaps it was so that they could see that if he could forgive this person, that they could and should as well
* Perhaps it was so that the church could have stronger unity and did not have to take sides in a conflict

2:11

* To not provide forgiveness would be to give Satan some type of advantage over us
* Literally this says, "so that Satan may not take advantage of us"
* The word for "take advantage of" is the word *pleonekteó* (πλεονεκτέω) can also mean "defrauded". It is the idea of having something take from us that belongs to us
* To refuse forgiveness would be to give Satan a chance to take something from the Christian
* The thing that Satan threatens to take might be our joy, unity, blessing and ultimately their own forgiveness

- In Ephesians Paul also connect bitterness and unforgiveness to Satan gaining an advantage
    - **Ephesians 4:26-27** - [26] "In your anger do not sin": Do not let the sun go down while you are still angry, [27] and do not give the devil a foothold (NIV)
- Bitterness and division are tools that Satan uses to destroy the church and gain foothold
- Paul reminds the reader that they are not ignorant of the Devil's schemes
- The Devil's schemes can be seen many times through the pages of Scripture and we can learn from the mistakes of those who have gone before us
- Satan certainly has his own *modus operandi*
    - **Ephesians 6:11** - [11] Put on the full armor of God, so that you will be able to stand firm against the schemes of the devil.

- The word used for "schemes" in Ephesians 6 is the word *methodeia* from where we get our English word "method"

2:12-13

- This verse marks a transition between Paul's defense of his travel plans and his defense of his boldness
- Paul says that he came to the city of Troas
- The thing that brought him to the city of Troas was an opportunity to preach the Gospel
- We know that Paul had visited Troas on a couple of different occasions
    - **Acts 16:8-9** - [8] and passing by Mysia, they came down to Troas. [9] A vision appeared to Paul in the night: a man of Macedonia was standing and appealing to him, and saying, "Come over to Macedonia and help us."
    - **Acts 20:5-6** - [5] But these had gone on ahead and were waiting for us at Troas. [6] We sailed from Philippi after the days of Unleavened Bread,

> and came to them at Troas within five days; and
> there we stayed seven days.

- Paul says that "he had no rest for his spirit" which means that he had some level of anxiety about a report from Corinth and seeing Titus
- Previously, Paul had sent Titus to Corinth to straighten some things out
- Paul had hoped that he would meet back up with Titus at the city of Troas and get some type of report on the church's response
- Paul does not reveal the whole story of his meeting up with Titus
- However, he does make it clear that from Troas he travelled to Macedonia
- It was in Macedonia that he would meet up with Titus and find some relief
    - **2 Corinthians 7:5-6 -** [5] For even when we came into Macedonia our flesh had no rest, but we were afflicted on every side: conflicts without, fears within.

2:14

- Notice a shift in Paul's tone here
- He went from having an uneasy spirit to thanks to God
- Paul uses the metaphor of an ancient Roman triumph
- The word for "triumph" here is the Greek word *thriambeuó* (θριαμβεύω)
- An ancient triumph spoke of the marching of a victorious general and a conquered enemy into their city in a grand parade
- This concept would have been a well-known one to the original readers
- Ancient documents reveal the occurrence of over 350 such triumphs
- The general would parade his victorious army and the prisoners of war through the streets
- The focus is on all of the smells associated with this ancient triumph

- Ancients cities did not usually smell great to start with, which is why many wealthy people lived outside the cities
- However, the smell of the triumph was even more distinct
- You would have men coming back from war which would have had a certain smell of its own
- You would have had the animals that came with them
- You would have the flowers and the incense which would have been all throughout the parade
- You had the prisoners of war who might expect execution if not for some act of grace on the part of the leader
- It is said that they would burn huge censors of incense or spices to try to cover up the smell of these events which would have also produced a distinct smell
- William Barclay describes the Roman triumph this way: To attain it he must satisfy certain conditions. He must have been the actual commander-in-chief in the field. The campaign must have been completely finished, the region pacified and the victorious troops brought home. Five thousand of the enemy at least must have fallen in one engagement. A positive extension of territory must have been gained, and not merely a disaster retrieved or an attack repelled. And the victory must have been won over a foreign foe and not in a civil war. In a Triumph the procession of the victorious general marched through the streets of Rome to the Capitol in the following order. First came the state officials and the senate. Then came the trumpeters. Then were carried the spoils taken from the conquered land. For instance, when Titus conquered Jerusalem, the seven-branched candlestick, the golden table of the shew-bread and the golden trumpets were carried through the streets of Rome. Then came pictures of the conquered land and models of conquered citadels and ships. There followed the white bull for the sacrifice which would be made. Then there walked the captive princes, leaders and generals in chains, shortly to be flung into prison and in all probability almost immediately to be executed. Then came the lictors bearing their rods, followed by the musicians with their lyres; then the priests swinging their censers with the sweet-smelling incense burning in them. After that came the general

himself. He stood in a chariot drawn by four horses. He was clad in a purple tunic embroidered with golden palm leaves, and over it a purple toga marked out with golden stars. In his hand he held an ivory sceptre with the Roman eagle at its top, and over his head a slave held the crown of Jupiter. After him rode his family; and finally came the army wearing all their decorations and shouting Io triumphs! their cry of triumph. As the procession moved through the streets, all decorated and garlanded, amid the cheering crowds, it made a tremendous day which might happen only once in a lifetime."

- When Paul picks up on this imagery, notice who it is that does the leading of this triumph
- It is God in Christ who leads the triumph as a conquering general
- The question is, in this image who are Paul and the apostles?
- Are they the victorious army or are they the captives?
- The word "triumph" actually spoke of simply the leading of the conquered army in a parade
- This is the way that same word was used in the book of Colossians
    - **Colossians 2:15** - [15] When He had disarmed the rulers and authorities, He made a public display of them, having triumphed over them through Him.
- In other words, in the imagery, Paul is not a soldier of the victorious army. He is not the conquering general. He is the one who is conquered and is now imprisoned
- It seems that the idea is that Christ is leading Paul (and the other apostles) in this victory march as a servant who has been set free from the sentence of death, but is a willing servant
- Paul said a similar thing in 1 Corinthians
    - **1 Corinthians 4:9** - [9] For, I think, God has exhibited us apostles last of all, as men condemned to death; because we have become a spectacle to the world, both to angels and to men.
- The purpose of a triumph was to flaunt the power of the victor
- Here, the idea is to show the power of God through the conquered people

- One of the questions that is center stage in both Corinthian letters is Paul's suffering
- Evidently, some Corinthians would have interpreted Paul's suffering as weakness and would have used that to question his apostleship
- Here, Paul is saying that God's power is on display through him in this whole thing
- He is not the one to be celebrated, but he is the agency in which Christ is lifted up
- Paul says that the "aroma" of the knowledge of Him is manifested through him
- Notice the scope of this particular triumph
- This triumph is not a one day thing
- Paul says that "God always leads us" in triumph
- This triumph is not a one place thing
- Paul says that it is in "every place"

2:15-16

- In the previous verse, the word "fragrance" is used. That word is a neutral word which simply speaks of some type of smell
- Here, the word "aroma" is used which is a word that speaks of a good smell
- Paul is not the source of the smell
- He says that they are the aroma of Christ
- He is claiming that the aroma that he gives off is that of Jesus
- The good smell comes from the preaching of the Gospel
- The language here reminds us of the sacrifices
- In the Old Testament, sometimes the sacrifices would be described as a "fragrant aroma to God"
- Paul says that the aroma that he gives off from his preaching of the Gospel is one that goes to God
- In fact, he says that he is the aroma of Christ to God
- It is not just that the aroma goes to other people, it is also that the aroma goes to God
- Paul's aim is to be pleasing to God first and foremost
- His preaching of the Gospel is a sort of sacrifice

- The aroma also is something around the people in the world
- He is saying here that the aroma of the Gospel is among all people
- It is among both those who are being saved and among those who are perishing
- He says that he is the fragrance of Christ meaning he is spreading the message of Christ to the world, but the work of this also goes up to God as a pleasing aroma
- Paul contrasts the aroma that his preaching of the Gospel gives off to two different groups
- The first group is those who are being saved
- The second group is those who are perishing
- How you interpreted this smell would depend upon which side you were on
- The smell did not change, but the way it was viewed changed depending on the person
- He describes that to the saved that he is giving off the aroma of life to life
- However, to the perishing he gives the aroma of death to death
- It might not be surprising the perishing would feel that Paul smells of death since the message of his preaching was Jesus Christ and him crucified
- Also, the perishing might regard that Paul smells of death because he spoke of himself being given over to death for Him

- The Greek idiom death to death or life to life speaks of it being an ever increasing thing
- This same type of idiom is used elsewhere in the New Testament
  - **2 Corinthians 3:18** - [18] But we all, with unveiled face, beholding as in a mirror the glory of the Lord, are being transformed into the same image from glory to glory, just as from the Lord, the Spirit.
  - **Romans 1:17** - [17] For in it *the* righteousness of God is revealed from faith to faith; as it is written, "But the righteous *man* shall live by faith."
- If you were on the side of the victors, that pungent smell was good. It represented life. It represented that your people lived

through a battle or war. It was a triumph

- If you were on the side of the victor, the reminder was that things are good and they are going to get better
- If you were on the side of the defeated, the smell was a further reminder of death and defeat. The smell would have indicated to the vanquished that things were bad and they were going to only get worse
- Those who reject the gospel are spiritually dead now, but they are continually dying and it will only get worse as time moves on
- Those who accept the gospel are alive now, but their situation will continue to get only better as time goes on
- The cross can only be seen to represent death and weakness to the lost
- However, to the saved, the cross reminds us of real life

2:17

- Paul wants to put to rest any thought that he is doing what he does for some type of personal gain
- He suggests that there are many people that do preach the Gospel as though they are "peddling the word of God"
- To peddle the Word of God is to treat the Gospel like a product to sell
- The word "peddle" is the Greek word *kapéleuó* (καπηλεύω) which means to hawk, trade or make a deal for the purpose of gain
- This does not necessarily speak to the content that was preached, but the motives of the one preaching it
- Paul made clear that some people did not have pure motives
    - **Philippians 1:15-17** - [15] It is true that some preach Christ out of envy and rivalry, but others out of goodwill. [16] The latter do so out of love, knowing that I am put here for the defense of the gospel. [17] The former preach Christ out of selfish ambition, not sincerely, supposing that they can stir up trouble for me while I am in chains. [18] But what

> does it matter? The important thing is that in every
> way, whether from false motives or true, Christ is
> preached. And because of this I rejoice.

- Paul points to his sincerity
- Further, he says we speak the Gospel from God, in Christ, and in God's sight
- This helps us to understand what he was saying in verse 15 when he said "we are the fragrance of Christ, to God"
- Here, the idea is that God can testify that His preaching was from pure motives
- Paul did not profit from the preaching of the Gospel

2 Corinthians 3

3:1

- The idea commending ourselves sounds a bit like someone who is being boastful or arrogant
- In fact, the presence of the word "again" implies that someone has accused him of being boastful or criticized him for commending himself
- Notice also that there is a plural used
- It is not just Paul, but it is "ourselves"
- It very well could be speaking of the apostles as a group
- This issue of commending will be an issue that will be present often in 2 Corinthians
- Commendation in the ancient world spoke of friendship and recommendation
- We would say that they would have understood "self-commendation" to be "self-introduction"

- It was the way that a person introduced himself to someone without a go between to do the introducing
- Letters of introduction were a common thing in the ancient world
- Anyone with a letter of commendation from a mutual friend would likely find acceptance
- The letter of introduction was like a reference on a resume
- Paul is asking the Corinthians if their relationship is such that he needs to have other people write some letter of introduction for him or does he need to give to convincing argument that he is trustworthy
- Notice that he suggests says "like some"
- The some who had letters of introduction were those who were causing the issues at Corinth
- It is probable that some false teachers were present in Corinth who had slandered Paul and perhaps came with their own letters of introduction
- We do not know the identity of this group
- Perhaps they were some Judaizers who came to Corinth with some type of commendation from well-respected leaders somewhere

3:2

- Paul suggests that he does not need a letter of commendation because the church at Corinth is his letter of commendation
- In place of an actual letter written on paper, Paul suggests the letter is written in their own hearts
- This letter is an open letter. It is visible for everyone to see and read
- It seems somewhat strange that the letter is said to be written on Paul's own heart and not the hearts of the Corinthians
- It was the person who was being recommended who carried the letter of recommendation
- Paul is saying that he carries in his heart evidence of his recommendation, which was the result of his work
- If Paul's opponents wanted a letter of commendation, the

Corinthians themselves are that letter
- Look at the beauty of Paul's argument: they would not be able to question the legitimacy of Paul as a result of this without calling into question the legitimacy of their own faith

3:3

- Paul describes more of this letter of commendation that was written on his own heart
- He will speak of four aspects of this letter
- First, he says that the author of the letter is Christ
- Paul is not just asserting his own authority
- Paul is saying that the Corinthians are proof of Christ's approval of his own work and ministry
- Second, he says that the one to deliver the letter is Paul and his companions
- Some versions say, "the result of our ministry"
- I believe the idea is of a letter bearer
- Third, he says that this letter is not written in ink, but by the Spirit of the living God
- If it is written by the Spirit of the Living God, the message does not fade like ink might
- The letter, which is the Corinthians speaks of their changed and converted lives
- Fourth, he says not on tablets of stone, but on human hearts
- If we follow the contrast, we might expect Paul to say that the letter was written not on paper or papyrus, however, he says "tablets of stone"
- The metaphor switches from talking about letters of commendation to the New Covenant versus the Old Covenant
- We must remember that the Old Testament Law was written on tablets of stone by God Himself
    - **Exodus 31:18** - [18] When He had finished speaking with him upon Mount Sinai, He gave Moses the two tablets of the testimony, tablets of stone, written by the finger of God.
- The idea Paul is conveying has to do with how the Law is

known
- It is not the writer that changes. It is the place where the thing that is written has changed
- God's Law has changed from being written on stones to on the heart
- A similar imagery is found in the book of Ezekiel
  - **Ezekiel 11:19-20** - [19] And I will give them one heart, and put a new spirit within them. And I will take the heart of stone out of their flesh and give them a heart of flesh, [20] that they may walk in My statutes and keep My ordinances and do them. Then they will be My people, and I shall be their God.
- The tablets of stone in Ezekiel refer to the hardness of the hearts of the people
- In the Old Covenant, God's work was primarily through the Law. In the New Covenant, we see the working of God inside of a person…in their heart
- In the Old Testament, God promised that one day He would write His Law on the hearts of man
  - **Jeremiah 31:33-34** - [33] "But this is the covenant which I will make with the house of Israel after those days," declares the Lord, "I will put My law within them and on their heart I will write it; and I will be their God, and they shall be My people. [34] They will not teach again, each man his neighbor and each man his brother, saying, 'Know the Lord,' for they will all know Me, from the least of them to the greatest of them," declares the Lord, "for I will forgive their iniquity, and their sin I will remember no more."
- This does not mean that every person knows the laws of God in their heart. They still have to learn them from the Word of God
- However, it does speak of the fact that the New Covenant carries the idea of heart transformation
- The point is that the Old Covenant worked externally while the New Covenant works from the inside out
- A Jew entered the Old Covenant at birth and then spent their life

learning the Law and about the covenant they entered into
- In the New Covenant, we learn about the terms of the covenant before we enter into it. It is a covenant people choose to enter into. It is through a spiritual birth.
    - **Matthew 28:19-20** - [19] Go therefore and make disciples of all the nations, baptizing them in the name of the Father and the Son and the Holy Spirit,[20] teaching them to observe all that I commanded you; and lo, I am with you always, even to the end of the age."
- Paul is emphasizing that his work is that of an apostle, working through Christ to create more than just a Law for people to memorize, but actual life transformation

3:4-5

- The key word in verses 4 and 5 is the word "confidence"
- Paul did not deny that he had confidence regarding his role as an apostle
- Paul says that any confidence he has about himself or his own adequacy is rooted in Christ, not in himself
- Any confidence Paul had in himself has been removed in Christ
    - **Philippians 3:3-6** - [3] for we are the *true* circumcision, who worship in the Spirit of God and glory in Christ Jesus and put no confidence in the flesh, [4] although I myself might have confidence even in the flesh. If anyone else has a mind to put confidence in the flesh, I far more: [5] circumcised the eighth day, of the nation of Israel, of the tribe of Benjamin, a Hebrew of Hebrews; as to the Law, a Pharisee;[6] as to zeal, a persecutor of the church; as to the righteousness which is in the Law, found blameless.
- Paul's confidence did not come from his past religious resume, his connections, his passions, his knowledge or his abilities
- While Paul is pointing to his adequacy as an apostle and teacher, he wants them to understand that he is adequate because God

made him adequate not because of his own ability

3:6

- Here, Paul describes that God is the one that made them adequate for the work they were called to do
- The way he describes his role is as a servant of the New Covenant
- In 2 Corinthians 2:16, Paul asks the question, "who is adequate for these things?"
- In that verse, he was speaking of his adequacy to be an apostle who was being led in a triumph as a captive or servant
- The answer to the question is 2:16 is that he is adequate because God made him adequate
- He did not become adequate for this incredible role on his own
- He was not voted adequate
- God made him adequate for the role as a servant
- The role of a servant of the New Covenant was to his job of spreading the message of the New Covenant
- Paul then makes a comparison between two things
- He compares the letter to the Spirit
- When Paul speaks of the "the letter" he is speaking of two things
- First, he is speaking of the Old Testament Law
- Second, he is speaking of people regarding the laws themselves as more important than the One who gave the laws and results in a legalism of law keeping without the heart
- The Old Testament Law certainly leant itself to this type of interpretation and application
- Jesus attempted to draw the hearts of people away from the mere letter of laws and to the spirit of the laws
- He said, "you have heard it said...but I say to you"
- The Pharisees often kept the laws without their hearts ever being sincerely engaged
- They obeyed out of duty and obligation, not because they wanted to or because they loved God
- Jesus claimed that his words were spirit and life
    - **John 6:63** - [63] It is the Spirit who gives life; the flesh

profits nothing; the words that I have spoken to you are spirit and are life.

- In Romans, Paul used the phrase "letter of the Law" to speak of external obedience without internal devotion
    - **Romans 2:26-29** - [26] So if the uncircumcised man keeps the requirements of the Law, will not his uncircumcision be regarded as circumcision? [27] And he who is physically uncircumcised, if he keeps the Law, will he not judge you who though having the letter *of the Law* and circumcision are a transgressor of the Law? [28] For he is not a Jew who is one outwardly, nor is circumcision that which is outward in the flesh.[29] But he is a Jew who is one inwardly; and circumcision is that which is of the heart, by the Spirit, not by the letter; and his praise is not from men, but from God.
- The New Covenant was intended to reach the heart of individuals in a way that the Old Covenant could not
- Paul points out the different results of letter and Spirit
- We get a glimpse of what Paul meant by "letter" when he says that the "letter kills"
- It is my understanding that when Paul speaks of "letter" here he is speaking of the inability of the Old Testament Law to penetrate the heart of people versus the ability of the New Covenant to change the heart and transform the life

3:7

- Here, Paul refers to the Old Testament Law as being a "ministry of death"
- This is an explanation of how the letter kills
- The letter (or law) kills and is a ministry of death because its purpose was to reveal to people that they are law breakers
    - **Romans 5:20** - [20] The Law came in so that the transgression would increase; but where sin increased, grace abounded all the more

- The Law brings death because the Law prescribes death for those who break the Law
- Sin is breaking the law of God. The wages of sin is death (Romans 6:23)
- So, the law establishes every person that has broken any law at any time as a lawbreaker deserving of death
- Paul says that this ministry that brought death came with glory
- The problem was not the Law itself. The Law was a good thing.
  - **Romans 7:7-12** - [7] What shall we say then? Is the Law sin? May it never be! On the contrary, I would not have come to know sin except through the Law; for I would not have known about coveting if the Law had not said, "You shall not covet." [8] But sin, taking opportunity through the commandment, produced in me coveting of every kind; for apart from the Law sin *is* dead. [9] I was once alive apart from the Law; but when the commandment came, sin became alive and I died; [10] and this commandment, which was to result in life, proved to result in death for me; [11] for sin, taking an opportunity through the commandment, deceived me and through it killed me. [12] So then, the Law is holy, and the commandment is holy and righteous and good.
- Paul is setting up a "how much more" argument
- He is calling his reader's minds back to the specific event of the Law being delivered to Moses at Mount Sinai
- Paul says that the ministry of death came with glory
- It did not just come with some glory, it came with great glory
- The giving of the Law was a glorious moment
- Paul will remind the readers of the incredible events surrounding the reception of this Law
- Paul was an Old Testament scholar. So, he uses an Old Testament story to teach a brand new truth to the Corinthians
- The truth is not about the Law and its reception
- The readers would have known that the Law came with glory
- The glory of the Lord rested on Mount Sinai

- - **Exodus 24:16-18** - [16]The glory of the Lord rested on Mount Sinai, and the cloud covered it for six days; and on the seventh day He called to Moses from the midst of the cloud. [17]And to the eyes of the sons of Israel the appearance of the glory of the Lord was like a consuming fire on the mountain top. [18]Moses entered the midst of the cloud as he went up to the mountain; and Moses was on the mountain forty days and forty nights.
- They also would have known about Moses' face shining in reflection of God's glory
- When Moses came down from Mount Sinai his face was glowing
- His face was reflecting the glory of God that he had seen pass by
  - - **Exodus 34:29-30** - [29]It came about when Moses was coming down from Mount Sinai (and the two tablets of the testimony *were* in Moses' hand as he was coming down from the mountain), that Moses did not know that the skin of his face shone because of his speaking with Him. [30]So when Aaron and all the sons of Israel saw Moses, behold, the skin of his face shone, and they were afraid to come near him.
- The point will not be a defense of the Law and its glory
- The point will be that if the Law brings death (and it does) and it came with glory, how much greater glory is there for the thing that brings real life
- Notice what Paul says about the glory that came with the Old Covenant
- Paul says that the glory was fading
- With the passing of time, the glory that was on Moses' face began to fade
- The word translated "fading" is the Greek word *katargeo* (καταργέω) which means, rendered inoperative, abolished or replaced by a more complete version of a similar thing
- The same word was used in 1 Corinthians 13:8 to describe how the gift of prophecy will be "done away with" or replaced by a completed version of it

- Paul uses this to teach that the Old Covenant was never intended to be permanent
- The Law only had glory for a season

3:8

- Paul's point is that if the thing that resulted in death came with glory, shouldn't we assume that the thing that brings life does as well
- The Old Covenant brought death. The New Covenant brought life
- The Old Covenant was temporary. The New Covenant is permanent
- Paul says that the New Covenant has even more glory

3:9

- Previously, Paul called the Old Testament Law a ministry of death. Now, he calls it a ministry of condemnation
- The point is that the consequences of Law breaking are not merely physical death, but they include spiritual death
- This does not mean that every person under the Law faced eternal condemnation
- The point is that by the strictest standards of the law, the penalty for being a law breaker is eternal condemnation
- Paul says that the Law of Moses which was powerless to save
    - **Romans 8:3** - For what the law was **powerless** to do because it was weakened by the flesh, God did by sending his own Son in the likeness of sinful flesh to be a sin offering

- The law could never set a person free from sin and death
- It was not that the law was weak in itself. It was flesh of man that is pointed out as being weak
- The law was only weak because the law could not be perfectly kept by man
- And once that law was broken it could not deliver in any way.

There were no provisions for deliverance for lawbreakers
- The only way for God to relate to us in a righteous (and just) way once we have broken the law, is to satisfy the law's requirement of punishment (death)
- The substitutionary death of Jesus takes care of this
- The New Covenant is referred to as a ministry of righteousness
- The New Covenant does not reduce the moral code to such that people are more likely to keep it
- In fact, Jesus raised the bar from not just outward obedience, but also matters of the heart
- So, in what way is the New Covenant a ministry of righteousness?
- There are two ways that the new covenant is a ministry of righteousness
- First, the New Covenant is a ministry of righteousness because Jesus paid the penalty for us
- It is a ministry of righteousness in that a right standing with God is made available through it
    - **Romans 1:16-17** - [16] For I am not ashamed of the gospel, for it is the power of God for salvation to everyone who believes, to the Jew first and also to the Greek. [17] For in it *the* righteousness of God is revealed [i]from faith to faith; as it is written, "But the righteous *man* shall live by faith."
- Paul says that the Gospel has the power of salvation
- The Gospel is the cause. Salvation is the effect
- Paul is NOT saying that in the Gospel it is revealed that God is righteous and that is why he is not ashamed
- This has nothing to do with the nature of God, although plenty of other Scriptures teach that God is righteous
- It also is not justification that he is talking about, in the sense of forgiveness
- Notice also it is a righteousness from God
- As opposed to what? As opposed to from self- or human righteousness which comes from law keeping
- This righteousness here means the righteousness which God imputes to us or credits to us

- Therefore, we are saved by having faith in God's righteousness imputed to us and not by our level of conformity to the law or by having personally satisfied the requirements of the law
- The word righteousness means "satisfying the requirements of the law"
- When we talk about law keeping or requirements of the law, we learn that none of us are perfect law keepers or perfectly righteous…so we can never be technically righteous. We do not meet that requirement.
- In the law there are commands to be obeyed and penalties to be paid for disobedience
- When we speak of the requirements of the law, it is not Jesus' doing that is credited to us, it is his dying
- The requirement that is credited to us is the credit of paying the punishment
    - **Colossians 2:12-14** - [12] having been buried with him in baptism, in which you were also raised with him through your faith in the working of God, who raised him from the dead. [13] When you were dead in your sins and in the uncircumcision of your flesh, God made you alive with Christ. He forgave us all our sins, [14] having canceled the charge of our legal indebtedness, which stood against us and condemned us; he has taken it away, nailing it to the cross.
- We are deemed as having already paid the penalty, not by being seen as without sin
- As a result of this gift of righteousness God treats us as if we had already paid sin's penalty which Jesus paid for us
- Second, the New Covenant is a ministry of righteousness because real inner transformation is available
- This seems to be where Paul will take this conversation throughout this chapter
- Paul will go on to say that the New Covenant has an ever-increasing glory, which speaks of our transformation to Christlikeness
- The thing that brings righteousness should be viewed as having a greater glory than the thing that brought condemnation

3:10-11

- This is an explanation of how the ministry of the Spirit, the New Covenant has so much greater glory than the Old Covenant
- The fading glory of the Old Covenant is nothing compared to the glory of the New Covenant
- Paul repeats the idea he has been working towards
- The thing that passed away had glory at one time
- The thing that remains has a continuing and increasing glory
- It seems likely that this was directed at some Judaizers in the church at Corinth
- The Judaizers would have emphasized the superiority of the Old Covenant and called for people to submit to the Old Covenant regulations as a part of their salvation
- However, Paul's point is that by failing to recognize that the Old Covenant was temporary and that it was always pointing towards the New Covenant that they were missing the glory of the New Covenant
- They would be missing out on the things that God intended for them to know and have

3:12

- This is the result of what he has said in verses 7-11
- We might say that the "therefore" extends to the end of this chapter
- This is the start of Paul's commentary on the "veil" of Exodus
- Paul speaks about the hope that he has
- The hope that he has refers to three different things
- First, the hope speaks of a future glory that comes through the New Covenant
- Second, it is a confidence that his ministry is even more glorious than Moses' ministry
- Third, it is the confidence that he has been set apart for the role of minister of the New Covenant
- When he speaks about "hope" he does not mean a mere wishful thinking, but a confident expectation

- The result of his confident expectation is a greater level of boldness
- The word boldness of speech is the Greek word *parrésia* (παρρησία)
- It does not just speak of bold action, it speaks of bold speech
- The question may be, in what speech is Paul referring to?
- Certainly this hope that he referred to can refer to his speaking the Gospel so boldly in the face of opposition'
- He also is able to speak boldly in his correction of doctrinal errors and character issues in the church because of this
- Part of the issue the Corinthians had with Paul was the severity of his letter and the nature of his visit
- David Garland said of the phrase boldness of speech, it is "better understood in this context as referring to the right to speak freely and openly and to give frank criticism to cultivate moral improvement."
- It is referring to "freedom to speak" or not pulling any punches
- He is telling the Corinthians that he speaks so boldly to them in order to bring about their repentance
- Paul is saying that he speaks boldly because he is confident of his role
- Paul is not attempting to tear down Moses, but he is letting them know that just as God chose Moses to be a minister of the Old Covenant, He has called Paul to be a minister of the New Covenant
- Remember, he began this chapter by speaking about his confidence and adequacy as an apostle

3:13

- Here, Paul makes a contrast between himself (and the other apostles) and Moses
- The way that Paul is not like Moses is that his face is not veiled
- There must be some connection between the use of the phrase "boldness of speech" in verse 12 and the concept of the "veil" which will continue through this chapter
- Simon Kistemaker suggests that the Syriac (a dialect of

Aramaic) translation of verse 12 be considered. It says, "we behave ourselves with an uncovered eye" or "to uncover the head" which would serve as a contrast to "veiling the face"

- The idea would be that he is saying that "we behave ourselves openly before God and man"
- This would certainly seem to fit alongside what Paul has been defending in this letter
- This also would make a logical connection between verses 12 and 13
- In this verse, Paul dives into the story of Exodus 34
- He reminds the readers of the fact that Moses wore a veil on his face after coming down from Mount Sinai
- Paul says that he worse the veil so that the Israelites would not look intently at what was fading away
- It seems that the veil was not worn because they could not look at the fading glory, it was there so that they would not
- In other words, it did not shine so brightly that the glory hurt their eyes
- The question that is debated here is: was the veil warn to hide something from the sons of Israel or to protect them
- It is possible that they could not look upon the glory of God because to behold the glory of God with their sin and hardness of heart would be a death blow
- The idea here speaks of the effect of the glory of God on hardened hearts
- The veil was in place because the Israelites could not behold God's glory because it would have been a death blow to them
- When Moses came down from Mount Sinai, with his face glowing, Aaron and the Israelites were afraid
  - **Exodus 34:30** - ³⁰ When Aaron and all the Israelites saw Moses, his face was radiant, and they were afraid to come near him.
- Why were Aaron and the Israelites afraid of what they saw? It must have been because of their sin
- The Rabbinic tradition was that the sin with the golden calf caused their inability to look at Moses' face
- In this case, the veil on Moses' face served a similar purpose to

the fence that was set up around the base of Mount Sinai itself
- So, we certainly see some element of the veil being word to protect the Israelites
- However, I believe that the veil was to both protect and to hide something
- It was also a punishment to them for their hard hearts
- The veil was to hide the glory of God from the people
- The veil was an act of judgment so that the nation of Israel would miss the blessing of seeing the glory
- In Exodus 34, when Moses came down from Mount Sinai, he read the Law to the people with an uncovered face
  - **Exodus 34:33-35** - [33] When Moses finished speaking to them, he put a veil over his face. [34] But whenever he entered the Lord's presence to speak with him, he removed the veil until he came out. And when he came out and told the Israelites what he had been commanded, [35] they saw that his face was radiant. Then Moses would put the veil back over his face until he went in to speak with the Lord.
- Something about the Israelites' response must have caused Moses to start wearing a veil when he was around the people
- In other words, Moses was not doing them a favor, he was punishing them for their hardness of heart
- Seeing the glory of God was intended to be a blessing for the people
- The glory of God could not be a blessing to people with a hardened heart
- It must have been the Israelites outright defiance and contempt for God's laws that caused Moses to wear a veil
- Also, once again we are reminded that this glory was fading away
- Some have suggested that Moses wore the veil to keep the Israelites from seeing the fact that the glory was fading and his goal was to conceal the temporary nature of the Old Covenant
- I have a hard time accepting that Moses was attempting to hide something from the people in any way
- It literally says, "the end of that which was being made

inoperative"

- Perhaps the veil was worn to keep people from seeing the temporary, fading nature of the Old Covenant
- If God's fading glory had this result, what would his full glory do?
- Paul's point is that they are not veiling the glory of God in order to protect people in sin or with a hard heart

3:14-15

- Rather than being allowed to behold continually the fading glory, Paul says that the minds of the children of Israel were hardened
- Paul says that the minds of the Israelites were hardened
- It was not that the Israelites were unable to understand something, it was that they chose not to recognize it
- God warned Isaiah that the people that he preached to would hear, but intentionally refuse to understand
    - **Isaiah 6:9-10** - [9] He said, "Go and tell this people: "'Be ever hearing, but never understanding; be ever seeing, but never perceiving.' [10] Make the heart of this people calloused; make their ears dull and close their eyes. Otherwise they might see with their eyes, hear with their ears, understand with their hearts and turn and be healed."
- Ezekiel was warned about a people who have ears to ear, but refuse to hear
    - **Ezekiel 12:2** - [2] "Son of man, you are living among a rebellious people. They have eyes to see but do not see and ears to hear but do not hear, for they are a rebellious people.
- For the Israelites the veil remained over their hearts speaks of a position in which they intentionally refused to see, accept, and appreciate the true glory of God
- Paul says that the people remain in the same condition in the day that he wrote
- The people he is speaking about is national Israel

- They refused to see and accept that the Old Testament Law was temporary and that it was pointing to Jesus
- The hardening of their mind and the veil of their hearts points to the fact that they were unable to see that the Old Covenant was pointing to Jesus
    - **John 5:39** - [39] You search the Scriptures because you think that in them you have eternal life; it is these that testify about Me
- They could not understand that the Old Covenant was fading away, that it was always temporary and that God's intent was that it would be replaced by the New Covenant
- Notice that there is a switch of where the veil is
- In verse 13, the veil was on Moses' face to keep the Israelites from looking
- Now, Paul says that they veil is over the hearts of Israel
- It is not the Old Covenant that is veiled, it is the Israelites' hearts
- Paul says that the veil remains at the reading of the Old Covenant Law
- It remains because they people refuse to see and accept the truth
- This explains why some of the Jews during the first century rejected Christ despite the overwhelming evidence
- They did not accept Christ because they did not want to
- The idea of "hardening" is the idea of only being able to say "no" to God
- In Romans Paul speaks about the Israelites being hardened
    - **Romans 11:7-8** - [7] What then? What the people of Israel sought so earnestly they did not obtain. The elect among them did, but the others were hardened, [8] as it is written: "God gave them a spirit of stupor, eyes that could not see and ears that could not hear,
    to this very day.
- For unbelieving national Israel, the Gospel is what hardened them even further…it made them mad

3:16

- Paul concludes that the veil is removed from their hearts when a person turns to the Lord
- Paul probably had in mind the fact that Moses' veil was removed when he went to speak with the Lord
    - **Exodus 34:34** - [34] But whenever Moses went in before the Lord to speak with Him, he would take off the veil until he came out; and whenever he came out and spoke to the sons of Israel what he had been commanded
- The idea of turning to the Lord is another way to speak of conversion
    - **1 Thessalonians 1:9** - [9] For they themselves report about us what kind of a reception we had with you, and how you turned to God from idols to serve a living and true God
- The way a person turns to the Lord is through Christ
- It was the hardness of their hearts that kept them from turning to the Lord
- Paul gives us a good picture of what the Jewish attitude was that caused their hearts to be veiled
    - **Galatians 1:13-14** - [13] For you have heard of my former manner of life in Judaism, how I used to persecute the church of God beyond measure and tried to destroy it; [14] and I was advancing in Judaism beyond many of my contemporaries among my countrymen, being more extremely zealous for my ancestral traditions.
- Paul shows us several things…
- First, he was more zealous for traditions than he was for God or the actual Word of God
- Second, he was a blasphemer and a violent man
    - **1 Timothy 1:13** - [13] even though I was formerly a blasphemer and a persecutor and a violent aggressor. Yet I was shown mercy because I acted ignorantly in unbelief
- Third, he saw the church as an enemy to be destroyed, which shows his lack of openness to the truth

- Fourth, he was quite confident in his own righteousness
  - **Philippians 3:6** - [6] as to zeal, a persecutor of the church; as to the righteousness which is in the Law, found blameless.
- Notice that Paul says that the "veil is removed". This is passive. It is something that God does
- As we have seen, the hardening of the heart is something that God does and a person does
- God further hardens the heart to punish for hard heartedness and rejection
- While the removal of the veil over the heart is pictured as something God does, it is done in response to a person turning to the Lord

3:17

- This verse is the transition verse to verse 18
- The point that Paul is making here is about the transformation that comes by way of the Holy Spirit
- He tells them that the Spirit of the Lord brings liberty
- The liberty that he is referring to is liberty from the Law

3:18

- This verse is the crescendo of this discussion about the veil
- Now, Paul says that "we all with unveiled face"
- That is our hearts are not hardened
- The veil had been taken away because we have turned to the Lord
- We remember that Moses wore a veil after coming down from Mount Sinai, but he took it off every time he went to be with the Lord
- He says that we are beholding in a mirror
- The idea of "the mirror" is the Word of God
  - **James 1:23-25** - [23] For if anyone is a hearer of the word and not a doer, he is like a man who looks at his natural face in a mirror; [24] for *once* he has looked

> at himself and gone away, he has immediately
> forgotten what kind of person he was. [25] But one who
> looks intently at the perfect law, the *law* of liberty,
> and abides by it, not having become a forgetful
> hearer but an effectual doer, this man will be blessed
> in what he does.

- Paul is suggesting that through Christ we are able to see the glory of God that the Israelites were kept from seeing and from what unbelieving Jews refused to see
- The thing that "we with unveiled faces" can see is the glory of the Lord
- In this context we should understand "glory" to speak about character
- His glory is that which we read about Him in the Word of God
- In other words, we can behold the character of God through the Word of God
- Not only that, but he says that we are transformed into the same image
- The same image as what? The image that we see in the mirror. That is the character of God
- Paul is saying that through this process of continually looking into the mirror of the Word of God, we start to look more like God
- Then he uses the idiom "from glory to glory"
- In chapter 2, he used the idiom "life to life"
- The idea is of some that is ever-increasing
- Our transformation or sanctification is an ever increasing thing, not an instantaneous thing
- Paul is saying that by continually beholding the character of God in the Word of God we are being transformed from one degree of glory to another
- Moses reflected the Lord's glory after he had been with the Lord
- We reflect God's glory after being with Him in His Word
- The Holy Spirit transforms us through the Word of God
- This transformation occurs by this process of beholding constantly in the Word of God
- Transformation into the image of God is the purpose of our

creation
- The purpose of our redemption is our sanctification
- The truth is that we become like what we look at lovingly for a long time
- We become transformed into the image of God by regularly being in and around the Word of God on a regular basis

2 Corinthians 4

4:1

- What is said here and in the first six verses of chapter 4 is closely tied to what was just said in the previous chapter
- Remember, chapter divisions were not a part of the original writing
- When Paul says "we" he is speaking of his apostolic ministry
- We are not ministers of the New Covenant in exactly the same way that Paul was a minister of the New Covenant
- Paul is comparing the apostolic office to that of Moses
- He says that his calling to be an apostle was an act of God's mercy
- When Paul says, "having this ministry" he is referring back to the reference to ministry of the New Covenant to which he was called
- In chapter 3, the ministry of the New Covenant was called a ministry of the Spirit (3:8) and a ministry of righteousness (3:9)
- He says that his understanding of his role causes him to not lose heart
- The word that is translated "lose heart" is the Greek word *ekkakeó* (ἐκκακέω) which means "weary", it can speak of discouragement, or reluctance
- However, here the idea is not of him not tiring, it is of his not being timid

- The idea here of "not losing heart" reminds us of the boldness which he spoke of in 3:12
- It is his confidence in his calling as an apostle that causes him to speak frankly and boldly at times

4:2

- Here, Paul will speak of three practices that he as an apostle has renounced
- First, he says that he has renounced "the things hidden because of shame"
- The contrast is between his boldness and the poor motives of others
- Paul's actions were open for the whole world to witness
- Second, he says that he has renounced "walking in craftiness"
- The word "craftiness" is the Greek word *panourgia* (πανουργία). It is a compound word which means, "every task"
- Philip Hughes says, "the man who practices *panourgia* (*pan + ergon*) is ready to do anything, up to every trick."
- It is an unscrupulous cunning that stops at nothing to achieve a selfish goal
- The idea is of people who may use secret plots
- The crafty person is the opposite of a person who is candid and walking with integrity
- Third, he says that he has renounced adulterating the Word of God
- In 2:17, he spoke of those who "peddle the Word of God"
- The word for "adulterate" means to "falsify" or to lure using bait
- It seems that the ancient world was full of suspicion of teachers or philosophers who did things for personal gain
- After having spoken of what practices he renounced, he then speaks of what he does do
- He says that he operates with a manifestation or a disclosure of the truth
- Paul is quite confident that he and his preaching can withstand whatever scrutiny might come from other people's consciences

- In other words, people can observe his life and his preaching and see that he is not a phony

4:3

- Paul comes back to the idea of the veil
- Paul may have been accused of preaching a Gospel that was in some way veiled or ineffective
- He says that if the Gospel is veiled in any way, shape or form it is veiled to the one who is perishing
- The idea here is that whenever the Gospel is preached, the hearer is presented with two choices: accept it or reject it
- Paul is arguing that some people choosing to reject the Gospel does not make the Gospel un-true
- One person said, "The sun does not cease to be the sun although the blind do not see it."
- The veil is a metaphor of a hard heart
- The point is that it was not an issue with the Gospel, it was an issue of the hearer
- The Gospel is a scandal and foolishness to those who want to reject it
    - **1 Corinthians 1:23** - [23] but we preach Christ crucified, to Jews a stumbling block and to Gentiles foolishness
    - **Romans 9:33** - [33] just as it is written, "Behold, I lay in Zion a stone of stumbling and a rock of offense, And he who believes in Him will not be disappointed."
- Some people's hearts are veiled to the Gospel because the Gospel offends them
- The idea of one man dying for the salvation of the whole world and the idea of totally surrender to Christ is an idea so difficult for the veiled heart to accept
- In chapter 2, Paul said that to the perishing they are "the smell of death to death"

4:4

- He will seek now to describe the hearts and minds of the perishing whose hearts are veiled
- He says, that the "god of this world" has blinded the minds of the unbelieving
- The god of this world (or age) speaks of Satan
- Jesus referred to Satan at the Prince of this world
  - **John 12:31** - [31] Now judgment is upon this world; now the ruler of this world will be cast out.
- This is not ascribing deity to Satan
- Satan is referred to as the "god of this world" because he has some level of dominion
- Since he is referred to as "god of this age" that also implies that his power is limited and temporary
- The work of Satan upon the world cannot be ignored
- Some places the hardening of the heart is an action of the individual
- Some places the hardening of the heart is an act of judgment from God (Romans 11:7-8)
- Some places the hardening of the heart is the work of Satan
- I think it is safe to say that all three of those factor together
- The hardening of the heart takes places as a person rejects God, then God gets out of the way and lets Satan have his way
- In his death throes, Satan's goal is to thwart the work of God
- The effect of this is so that they might not see the light of the Gospel of the glory of Christ
- In other words, the veil which was over their hearts kept the people from seeing the glory of the Gospel in a similar way to the veil that Moses wore kept the people from seeing the glory of God
- Sometimes we wonder how people can reject what appears to us to be such plain, reasonable, logical truths
- This helps to explain why some people cannot see the logical truth of the Gospel

4:5

- While Paul may have to spend significant time defending his apostleship, he is reminding his readers that the object of his preaching is not himself or any other person

- Paul says his focus is two things
- First, his focus in preaching is Jesus Christ as Lord
- The Gospel is not about Paul, it is about Jesus as Lord
- Paul was opposed to any preaching which would have elevated the preacher over Christ
- Good, Biblical preaching is Jesus-centric
- For one to preach themselves would lead people to follow a preacher and not Jesus
- Second, his focus is on him being a bond-servant to others for Christ's sake
- There are several instances of Paul referring to himself as a slave of Christ
    - **Romans 1:1** - Paul, a bond-servant of Christ Jesus, called *as* an apostle, set apart for the gospel of God
    - **Philippians 1:1** - Paul and Timothy, bond-servants of Christ Jesus,
- This is the only instance of him referring to himself as a slave to other people
- Paul did not spend time puffing up his qualifications
- He saw himself as a servant to others
- The word translated "bond-servant" speaks of a slave
- Paul does not mean that he is like an employee of the church who is their "yes man", but he is one who is ministering to the spiritual needs of the church

4:6

- This is the answer to why he proclaims Christ as Lord and himself as bond-servant
- When Paul said, "God said, let light shine out of darkness" it is likely that he had two Scriptures in mind: Genesis 1:3 and Isaiah 9:2
    - **Genesis 1:3** - [3] Then God said, "Let there be light"; and there was light.

- o **Isaiah 9:2** - The people who walk in darkness Will see a great light; Those who live in a dark land, The light will shine on them.
- Paul is connecting the language of creation to the language of conversion
- His point is that his life and preaching shine forth the light of the Gospel
- The idea of "the light" has the idea of someone becoming aware of something
- So, when Paul speaks of "the light of the knowledge of the glory…" he is speaking of the fact that his life and preaching bring people to an awareness and a knowledge of the glory of God
- However, Paul says that the knowledge of the glory of God is found in the face of Jesus Christ
- Remember, in the previous verse, Paul declared that in his preaching his focused on Jesus as Lord
- He focused on Jesus as Lord because it is in his face that the glory of God is seen
- He is telling them, that it is not in Moses' face that one sees the glory of God. His face only gave a passing glance at the fading, reflected glory of God
- Jesus is not a mere reflection of God's glory, but he is the real thing
- Paul focused his preaching on Jesus as Lord because it is through Jesus that we can see the character (glory) of God

4:7

- Paul now speaks of having a treasure in earthen vessels
- The earthen vessels speaks about the apostles
- The treasure speaks of the light of the Gospel
- Paul is pointing to himself as a vessel who carries and proclaims the message of the Gospel
- I believe that there are several things that we can take away from the image of himself being an earthen vessel
- First, the idea of an earthen vessel carries the idea of something

fragile
- The Gospel does not need us to move forward
- Second, the earthen vessel is the idea of something that is ordinary, but inside of it resides something extraordinary
- Third, the emphasis is on his own human weakness
- Fourth, the earthen vessel really does not in itself offer any real protection to the thing inside it
- Fifth, the earthen vessel is not of great value
- The picture is not of some fancy stone or jewel, it is of cheap pottery
- There is a contrast which intends to point to the value of the thing inside the vessel
- The vessel was never intended to be the thing that stopped and grabbed every person's attention
- The vessel was always just a holder of the real treasure
- Paul answers why God's plan was to put this incredible treasure in an earthen vessel rather than in something more valuable
- The reason is so that the surpassing greatness of the power will be of God and not from ourselves
- In other words, it was so that the focus would not be on the vessel, but on the treasure
- No one looking at him would be impressed, but when they hear the Gospel they might be amazed that something so powerful could come from someone so weak
- The purpose of the earthen vessel is to carry the treasure
- The focus was never intended to be on the vessel, but rather the treasure
- It is not and it never will be about us…our lives should carry forth the treasure of the Gospel

4:8-9

- Here, Paul lists four ways in which he has faced opposition or difficulty
- There are other occasions where Paul lists his sufferings
- In each of these cases, he mentions that the actual result was different than what could have been the result

- First, he says, we are afflicted in every way
- Earlier, he spoke of affliction he faced in Asia (1:8)
- We might expect that in light of being afflicted in every way that they might be crushed or defeated
- Paul says, "we are not crushed"
- The word "crushed" means "pressed or confined"
- He is saying that his will and desire are not crushed out
- Perhaps this goes back to the idea of the breakable, fragile clay earthen vessels
- Despite being apparently fragile and facing outward pressure, they did not break
- Second, he says, we are perplexed
- The Greek word for perplexed is *aporeo* (ἀπορέω) which literally means to have no resources
- The idea is to be at a loss or to be at wits end
- He says that he is not despairing
- The word used for despairing is a similar word to the word "perplexed"
- He is saying, "I am perplexed, but not to the point of being overly perplexed" or "I am at a loss, but not totally at a loss"
- Third, he says, we are persecuted
- We have many accounts of persecutions that Paul faced
- In chapter 11, he will recount some of his persecutions
- He may be persecuted, but he is not forsaken
- He is especially not forsaken by God who promised to "never leave us or forsake us"
- Fourth, he says, we are struck down
- The word "struck down" means "laid low as by a weapon" or a knockdown in a boxing match
- He may be struck down, but he is not about to quit

4:10-11

- These verses summarize the idea that he has been teaching
- The point is how the death of Jesus is at work in himself while the life of Jesus is at work among the Corinthians
- When Paul speaks of "death" he does not use the usual word for

death (*thantos*), but uses the less common word (*nekrosis*) which describes the process of decomposition
- The focus here is on the suffering and death of Jesus
- Paul is saying that him and the other apostles experience the suffering of Jesus through the persecution they endure
- There is some similarity to Jesus' suffering and their present suffering
- The difference is that the apostle's suffering was not vicarious, but the point is on their sharing a similar suffering
  - **Romans 8:36** - [36] Just as it is written, "For Your sake we are being put to death all day long; We were considered as sheep to be slaughtered."
- When Paul says, "we always carry around in our body" he means a few things
- First, he means that he is the earthen vessel who always brings forth the message of Jesus' suffering and death
- Second, he saying that his body is being used for the spread of the Gospel and that includes facing suffering in his own body
- Paul's own sufferings are a constant carrying around of the death of Jesus
- Not only is the death of Jesus made known through their body, but the life of Jesus is as well
- Perhaps the idea of the life of Jesus being revealed is pointing to His resurrection from the dead

4:12

- Paul is saying that they face and endure suffering so that the Corinthians (and other churches) may hear the Gospel and be saved
- It is in this way that his suffering benefits the Corinthians

4:13

- Paul will continue to give an explanation for his continued boldness
- He quotes Psalm 116:10

- When the Psalmist wrote this, he, like Paul, was greatly afflicted
- The point the Psalmist makes is that he maintains his faith in God through affliction
- Paul says, "with the same spirit of faith" which means that he shares the attitude of the Psalmist
- The question is, how is it that he keeps speaking in face of persecution and opposition
- The answer is: he believes what he is preaching is true
- The basis for Paul's boldness to speak comes from the fact that he wholeheartedly believes the Gospel is true
- He is saying, "we believe, therefore we speak"

4:14

- Sometimes, even today, we have to ask ourselves why we do what we do
- The why is the reason we keep on going
- The why has the power to keep us going through difficult times
- For Paul, here he gives his why
- More specifically, Paul continues to speak boldly because of two things:
- One is that God raised Jesus from the dead
- Paul was motivated by a confidence that the resurrection of Jesus was a historical reality
- Second is that God will raise us also in the future
- The idea of a future resurrection is a core belief
- Jesus' resurrection is seen by Paul as an assurance of own future resurrection
- It is a motivation because he believes that a future resurrection also means a future judgment
- In other words, there is a sense of urgency connected to his message
- It is a motivation because he believes that a future resurrection means he is accountable to God
- There is a sense of responsibility he feels
- Notice the language of giving an account, "and present us with you"

4:15

- When he says, "all things are for your sake" the "all things" is the suffering that he has endured
- Paul has faced suffering because of his commitment to preach the gospel
- In a sense, that suffering could be said to be "for your sake"
- If he had not endured suffering the Corinthians (and many others) would have lost out on knowing Christ
- He says that as a result of all of this, grace is expanding to more and more people
- God's grace expands as more and more people are saved
- As a result of Paul's continued boldness, more and more people were coming to Christ
- The result of the expanding of God's grace is thanks being given to God
- Only a saved person can really give thanks to God
- Paul says that the ultimate goal of his ministry is to bring glory to God
- The goal of evangelism is to bring God glory
- Eugene Peterson sums up this passage this way: "more and more grace, more and more people, more and more praise"

4:16

- The idea of "lose heart" means to lose heart to preach the Gospel
- The reason he does not lose heart is because he has a sincere belief in the Gospel, a belief in a future reward and a belief that the result is worth it
- He does not deny that his stand as a minister of the New Covenant is taking a toll on his body
- He acknowledges that the outer man is decaying or wasting away
- The "outer man" speaks about his physical body
- This is true for each and every person. Our bodies decay with age and time
- The inner man refers to the spiritual self

- The outer man and the inner man should be heading in opposite directions
- The outer man is winding down
- The inner man is growing in Christlikeness
- Paul is not advocating for some type of Greek dualism, but he is making clear that the effect of persecution on his physical body did not harm his spiritual standing
- The promise of the renewing of the inner man reminds us of Paul's words in Romans 8
    - **Romans 8:28** - [28] And we know that God causes all things to work together for good to those who love God, to those who are called according to *His* purpose.
- The way God works things out is the transformation of the inner man

4:17

- The "for" lets us know that this is an explanation of how the suffering he undergoes causes his inner man to be renewed day by day
- He begins by describing his afflictions with two words
- First, he says that they are light
- The afflictions are only light when compared to the thing gained at the end
- They were not literally "light"
- In fact, when Paul recounts his toil and suffering, it seems quite heavy
- If you have suffered, it is likely that the word "weight" is a good word to describe how you feel. In your pain and heartache, in your uncertainty and fear, in your trial it feels like a weight. I have heard many people describe their pain this way. When they can't find a good word to describe how they feel, the word weight often comes to mind.
- Second, he says that they are momentary
- The afflictions are momentary in view of eternity
- Persecution could only affect the outer man

- When one views things from a heavenly perspective, it changes everything
- The idea of eternal glory is that of his character in eternity
- He is not saying that his suffering is earning him a spot in Heaven
- Suffering does not cause the eternal glory, but it is a vehicle God uses to shape our character
- He is speaking of the fact that his eternal character is being developed through suffering and persecution
- He makes this incredible play on words. He uses the phrase "weight of glory". It is interesting. I don't think a coincidence that the Hebrew word for "glory" literally means "weight" or "heavy".
- Paul is making clear that future glory outweighs present suffering.
- It may not feel like it right now, but it is true.
- The key to not losing heart, is to believe this. It is to believe that glory weighs more than suffering.
- Paul is saying that when you put it all on the scale, when you put your suffering on one side and the promise of future glory on the other, glory is heavier than suffering
- Paul is suggesting there is coming a day when we will look back at all we suffered and think to ourselves…it was only light and it was only momentary.
- How do we know this? Only by faith in what God said

4:18

- It is important to understand the opposite of faith is not reason
- The opposite of faith is sight
- Here, in this context, the thing he can see by sight is the decaying of the outer man as a result of persecution
- Common sense might direct a person who sees this to stop doing what it is that causes the persecution in order to stop the decaying of the outer man
- However, Paul is suggesting that there is more to the equation
- There are things happening which we cannot see with the human

eye

- There are things that are happening in the midst of suffering that we can only see by faith
- The thing that we cannot see by sight is the renewing of the inner man
- Implicit in this statement is the idea that that the Corinthians criticism of Paul is evidence that they have fixed their eyes only on what they can see
- Suffering is very visible while spiritual growth cannot be quantified or measured
- Paul's argument is that it is wiser to be focused on the eternal thing even though it cannot be seen with the eye

2 Corinthians 5

5:1

- This is probably not the best division of a chapter
- Chapter 5 continues the thoughts presented at the end of chapter

4

- The discussion had been about the fact that Paul had continued to speak boldly in spite of affliction, suffering and persecution
- Here, he speaks to them about his view towards his earthly life and body
- He introduces the thought as something that they are already familiar with by saying, "for we know"
- The Corinthians already know and have been taught that their earthly body will fade away and that they will have a new body in Heaven
- The contrast here will be between the earthly and the heavenly
- The earthly refers to something temporary
- In eight verses Paul will use three different metaphors
    - A tent (vs. 1)
    - Clothing (vs. 2-4)
    - Home (vs. 6-8)
- The first metaphor he uses is that of a tent
- This metaphor was something that has been used in other ancient literature to speak about our lives
- It is somewhat interesting that Paul the tentmaker will use the metaphor of a tent to describe the nature of our physical bodies
- When Paul speaks of the earthly tent, he is speaking of the physical bodies that we all have currently
- In chapter 4, Paul used the phrase "outer man" to refer to the physical body (4:16)
- Paul poses the thought of the earthly tent being "torn down"
- The image is that of a tent being taken down
- It seems that at the forefront of Paul's mind is not just the idea of growing old and dying, but of someone killing him and him being a martyr
- The image of our bodies being like a tent conveys clearly the idea that our life is not permanent
- The image of a tent also reminds us how fragile life is
- The idea of the fragility of life is something that Paul referred to with the earthen vessels as well
- A tent is an easy structure to tear down
- The earthly tent being destroyed speaks of death

- When he says, "a building from God" he is conveying two different thoughts in contrast
- First, it is a spiritual body known as our resurrected body
- Second, it is an everlasting body
- The idea of it being a building from God indicates that it is more permanent than a tent
- A building is more stable and more difficult to tear down than a tent

5:2

- Paul makes clear that his greatest desire is for the heavenly house not the earthly tent
- We groan for our heavenly house because our earthly tent is filled with suffering and pain
- The word "groan" is the word *stenazó* (στενάζω). It is the idea of groaning because of pressure of being exerted forward like the forward pressure of childbirth
- William Baker described "groaning" as something in between positive and negative
- The groaning is a longing for Heaven mixed with a growing dissatisfaction with life in our earthly bodies
- Paul used the same idea in Romans about a hopeful longing for our eternal reward
    - **Romans 8:22-23 -** [22] For we know that the whole creation groans and suffers the pains of childbirth together until now. [23] And not only this, but also we ourselves, having the first fruits of the Spirit, even we ourselves groan within ourselves, waiting eagerly for *our* adoption as sons, the redemption of our body.
- Viewing our present condition in light of our eternal promise cause the inward groaning and longing for that future reward
- The groaning that we experience in this life is because we long for an eternal body that is free from suffering
- Without an understanding of the heavenly building, it would not change the condition of the earthly tent and the sufferings we

face, but it does change how we view it
- Without a hope of the heavenly building, there can be no real groaning

5:3

- When he says, "when we are clothed" he is speaking of being clothed with our future, resurrected bodies
- The phrase "found naked" speaks of being without a body of any type
- The word "naked" here is the Greek word "*gymnos*" from which we derive our English word "gymnasium".
- The very goal of Greek Platonic thought was to achieve some type of bodiless state
- Paul suggests that actually, God has in mind our spirit being clothed with a new, permanent, resurrected body

5:4

- This echoes the same idea of a longing for the new body which he expressed in verse 2
- He adds that he is burdened
- The being burdened speaks of the physical hardships he endured in Asia (1:8)
- He does not groan simply to shed the physical body, he groans to receive the new body
- Paul makes it clear that is hope is that the physical body would be replaced by the better, immortal body that we will get at our future resurrection

5:5

- Paul says that believers have been prepared for this very thing by God
- The thing that we have been prepared for is our mortal body being swallowed up by life
- The promise of a new body is something that has been in the plan of God from the very beginning

- Paul notes that the current indwelling of the Holy Spirit is a
  pledge that the promise of a new body is coming
- The word "pledge" is the word *arrabon* (ἀρραβών) which is a
  business term for a down payment, a surety or earnest money. It
  is an advance payment which guarantees the rest is to come
- The thing to come in the future is our new body

5:6

- Being of good courage is the opposite of losing heart
- The idea of "being at home in the body" speaks of living with
  our current, mortal bodies in this life or still being in our earthly
  tent
- We see the metaphor switches to the idea of a home
- He says that while we are still in this body, we are away from
  the Lord
- We are not actually away from the Lord since He is omnipresent
- However, we cannot be with the Lord in the same sense as we
  can be after our death
- The reason that we cannot be with the Lord in this body is
  because flesh and blood cannot inherit the kingdom of God (1
  Corinthians 15:50)

5:7

- Here, Paul gives a simple explanation which will help
  understand both the previous statement and the next statement
- How can they know and trust that our ultimate goal is to be
  home with the Lord and apart from these physical bodies? Only
  through faith.
- He calls upon the Corinthians to view their lives through the
  eyes of faith
- To walk by faith means to live by faith
- To walk by faith means to depend on the information that God
  has given us
- He wants them to walk by faith and confidence in the promise
  that God made of a new, better, immortal body

- The word for "sight" is a word that means "shape" or "form"
- The idea of walking by sight has to do with walking with only our physical bodies in view

5:8

- Paul says that he and his companions have good courage right now because they walk by faith and not by sight
- In other words, they have something beyond this life in mind
- Persecutors may be able to harm his physical body, but he knows that there is something better awaiting him which gives him courage to continue preaching
- To be absent from the body points to death
- At death, the physical body is left behind
- This is the same idea as the groaning or longing to be clothed
- Some have criticized Paul as being flippant about life by saying that he would rather be away from the body and home with the Lord
- Paul preferred to be absent from the body because the conditions after life in this body are better
- Our existence after death is better for two reasons
- First, it is better because we will have a better body
- Second, it is better because we will be with the Lord

5:9

- Paul points to the fact that his ultimate aim does not change regardless of whether he is in his physical body or in his eternal reward
- His aim, which should be every Christian's aim is to strive to please the Lord
- His goal is to please the Lord and not man

5:10

- The reason he is concerned about striving to please the Lord is that it is before the Lord that he must give an account

- The word judgment seat is the Greek word *"bema"*
- We are reminded that in the city of Corinth sat a *bema* where people would stand trial before a judge
- Paul wants the Corinthians to know that there is coming a future day when every person will stand before God's judgment seat
- There is no person who is exempt from this future judgment
- I believe that this points to the idea that there will be some future accounting for our deeds
- We are not judged to Heaven based on our good and bad deeds
- Our eternal destiny is determined based on whether or not we are in Christ
- However, we are rewarded based off of our good or bad deeds
- We will be give an account for the things that we did or did not do while we were in our physical bodies
- What we do with our bodies and while in our bodies matters

5:11

- The fear of the Lord has to do with the idea that we all must stand before the judgment seat of Christ
- The idea of giving account to God was something that Paul saw applying to himself
- Specifically, he understood that he would give an accounting to God for his ministry as an apostle of Christ
- The result of understanding this future accountability is the fear of the Lord
- The Biblical idea of "fearing the Lord" is not like a phobia, but it is a respectful fear that directs a person's life
- The fear of the Lord is an awareness of the fact that God is absolutely holy and awesome
- The fear of the Lord has a positive result not a crippling result
- Proverbs says that the fear of the Lord is the beginning of wisdom
  - **Proverbs 9:10** - The fear of the Lord is the beginning of wisdom, And the knowledge of the Holy One is understanding
- The writer of Ecclesiastes also connects the fear of the Lord with

the giving of an account

- o **Ecclesiastes 12:13-14** - [13] The conclusion, when all has been heard, *is*: fear God and keep His commandments, because this *applies to* every person. [14] For God will bring every act to judgment, everything which is hidden, whether it is good or evil.
- Paul says that on account of this fear of the Lord, he strives to persuade men
- There are two reasons that this serves as a motivation for Paul
- First, he wants to faithfully discharge the duties of his ministry and to fail to do so would be disobedience to the God to whom he will stand before in judgment
- Second, since all people will stand before the judgment seat of Christ, he does not want any person to have to give an account for disobedience or defiance
- The word "persuade" does not imply any type of scheme or trickery as he has already made clear
- For an unbeliever to become a believer they must be persuaded of the truth and logic of the message of the Gospel
- Persuasion is also necessary in dealing with false teachers or rebellious Christians who need to be corrected
- Persuasion is necessary for the erring sinner, who may need to be convinced that their behavior is indeed sinful
- Persuasion was necessary for any of Paul's critics who challenged his sincerity or the legitimacy of his calling
- It seems that when he says, "I hope that we are made manifest in your consciences" that he is saying that he hoped that the Corinthians are able to determine that his motives are pure

5:12

- Paul had already spoken of the idea of commending himself (3:1)
- To commend oneself does not mean anything about being boastful
- For Paul, commending means self-introduction

- The Corinthians do not seem to be accusing Paul of being boastful, in fact, they might suggest that he is not boastful enough
- Paul says that he wants to give the Corinthians an occasion to be proud of them
- That is that they should be proud of their association with Paul as an apostle
- The exact idea that he is conveying when he speaks of "taking pride" in them is that they would stand up for him before his critics
- His comments are an attempt to give the church a ready answer to Paul's critics
- The critics were those who took pride in the wrong things
- We do not know details about these critics, but he accuses them of taking pride in appearance
- This does not just mean physical appearance, but it would include all the external ways of coming to a conclusion about a person
- It is probable that Paul did not fit the cultural mold of someone that would have any pride taken in
- The difference is between those who look at appearances versus those who look at the heart
- The critics came to the wrong conclusion about Paul because they were using the wrong criteria to evaluate him

5:13

- Paul's statement here is a declaration that the things he does he does for God
- The phrase "beside ourselves" may give a clue as to what some of the critics were saying about Paul
- The accusation was likely that Paul was out of his mind or a bit eccentric
- He is saying that if people think that his actions are not normal, they should know that all that he has said and done was for God's sake
- He was not trying to impress or please his critics, he was doing

what God wanted him to do
- Then he says that if the conclusion is that he was in his right mind then it should be understood that what he did he did for the sake of the spiritual welfare of the church

5:14

- Here, Paul explains what it is that motivates him to continue preaching even though he faces opposition from inside and outside the church
- He says it is "the love of Christ" that controls and dictates his behavior
- It is not certain if Paul is speaking of his love for Christ, Christ' love for him or both
- He says that Christ's love controls him
- The Greek word for "control" is *sunecho* (συνέχω) which means "holds together" or "constrains"
- It seems most likely that the idea is that when Paul considers what God has done for him in Christ, he feels it leaves him with no other choice but to speak the Gospel
- This is seen by the fact that he defines the idea of the Gospel here
- He will speak first about his conclusion of what Jesus did for us and then what that means to our lives
- He says that they have concluded that one died for all
- The picture is of Jesus' vicarious death which serves to motivate Paul's preaching
- The one dying speaks of the fact that Jesus paid the penalty of death for all
- Jesus died for all the sins of all the world
    - **1 John 2:2** - and He Himself is the propitiation for our sins; and not for ours only, but also for *those of* the whole world.
- Jesus died for all people potentially and for the saved actually
- Second, he says that as a result of that "all died"
- When he says "all died" the idea is that in the mind of God all people in Christ paid the penalty for their sin which is death

- In Christ, because of Christ, all people have died as in their penalty is paid
- Also the idea Paul has in mind is that because Jesus died in our place, we have all died to ourselves and our own desires

5:15

- Here he repeats the idea that Christ's death for was all
- Now he speaks of a present, spiritual benefit to Christ dying on our behalf and us dying in the mind of God with Him
- When he speaks about those who live he is speaking of those who are alive in Christ because the penalty for their sin is paid
- He says that the ones who live no longer live to themselves
- This seems to be pointing specifically to the different life of a person who is a Christian
- Since we have died to ourselves and died to sin, we now live for Christ
    - **Colossians 3:3** - [3] For you have died and your life is hidden with Christ in God.
    - **Galatians 2:20** - [20] I have been crucified with Christ; and it is no longer I who live, but Christ lives in me; and the *life* which I now live in the flesh I live by faith in the Son of God, who loved me and gave Himself up for me.
- Once again, Paul points to the fact that Jesus death and resurrection was vicarious in that he died and rose "on their behalf"
- This is certainly true for all people, but also Paul was explaining why his preached in the face of opposition. He did so because he lives for Christ who died and rose on his behalf

5:16

- Because he does not live for himself, but lives for Christ, he views other people differently
- Literally it says, "no according to flesh"
- One of the major shifts in conversion should be the way that we

view other people
- The contrast is between how his critics view people and how they should view people
- In verse 12, he spoke of his critics who may take pride in appearances over the heart
- This is an example of "regarding one another according to the flesh"
- His critics were looking at appearances
- Perhaps Paul was guilty of this way of viewing other people before he was a Christian
- As a Jew, he likely regarded Gentiles according to the flesh
- As a Christian, Paul now views people through their relationship to Christ
- Paul concedes that his way of regarding people was wrong
- When we are Christians it should change the way we view other people
- As Christians there is no place for racism, judgment based on physical appearances and favoritism
- Paul says that they once regarded Christ according to the flesh
- This speaks of Paul's view of Jesus before he was a Christian
- If one were to use worldly criteria for determining success, they might see weakness in Jesus
- One of the difficulties skeptics had was how this one that people elevated and worshipped could have died a criminal's death
- The cross is really a scandal in that way
- To view Christ according to the flesh might be viewing him as simply being a good moral teacher
- To view Christ according to the flesh might be to reject His miracles
- To view Christ according to the flesh might be to challenge His claims
- To view Christ according to the flesh might be to question His deity
- To view Christ according to the flesh might be rejecting Him as the Messiah

- Here, we see that the change comes from being "in Christ"
- The term "in Christ" is a phrase that Paul uses quite frequently
- The phrase is used over twenty-five times in Paul's writings
- To be "in Christ" refers to a person being saved
- A person gets in Christ by uniting themselves with Christ
  - **Galatians 3:26-27** - [26] So in Christ Jesus you are all children of God through faith, [27] for all of you who were baptized into Christ have clothed yourselves with Christ.
  - **Romans 6:3-4** - [3] Or don't you know that all of us who were baptized into Christ Jesus were baptized into his death? [4] We were therefore buried with him through baptism into death in order that, just as Christ was raised from the dead through the glory of the Father, we too may live a new life.
- This points out that being in Christ should produce some very clear changes
- He points out several things that are different in Christ
- First, he says, he is a new creature
- The focus is that there is a vastly different character and perspective in Christ
- Second, he says "the old things have passed away"
- This literally means "the old has come and gone"
- Primarily what he means here is that at one point in time he viewed Jesus as just a man, but that old way of thinking has gone
- He now, as a Christian, views Jesus differently than he once did
- Third, he says "new things have come"
- Once again, this is a new character and new perspective

5:18

- When he says, "all this is from God", he means that the inner transformation is something that God is working in us
- In this context, the ones with the ministry of reconciliation speaks of the apostles

- It is true that all Christians have a ministry of reconciliation as well
- God is the one who does the reconciling. Man is the one who is reconciled
- For a reconciliation to occur we have to assume that the relationship has been damaged
- The problem was not with God, the problem was with man
- God did not need to be reconciled, we needed to be reconciled to Him
- When Paul says that God gave him a ministry of reconciliation he means that God has given him the responsibility to spread the message of reconciliation
- For a person to be reconciled to God they have to be aware of three things:
- First, they have to be aware of the fact that the relationship has been damaged or that there is a need to be reconciled
- Second, they have to desire for that relationship to be repaired
- Third, they have to know the terms of reconciliation or how to be reconciled
- Paul's role was to emphasize those three things

5:19

- Here we have the start of a description of the nature of this reconciliation
- Notice once again that the one doing the reconciling is God
- God did this reconciling through Christ
- The nature of this reconciliation is that God was not counting men's sin against them
- It is sometimes translated "reckoned" or "imputed"
- It is a banking term that means "to put into one's account"
- The word "counting" means "speaking"
- In other words, because God does not speak our sins against us
- Verse 21 will explain what happened to our sin in the mind of God
- Not only is righteousness imputed to us, but also our sin is imputed to Christ

- Reconciliation with God is based on imputation

5:20

- Paul proclaims that he is an ambassador for Christ
- This does not mean that every Christian is an ambassador in the sense that Paul is
- The idea of an ambassador is that an ambassador speaks with the full authority of a king
- The ambassador did not just speak for, but also in the place of
- Paul, here speaks of the apostles specifically being Christ's ambassadors
- Paul is saying that he (and the apostles) speaks with the full authority of the king
- Paul's words to them were words from an ambassador speaking with the authority of the king
- His words were the words of God
  - **1 Thessalonians 2:13** - [13] And we also thank God continually because, when you received the word of God, which you heard from us, you accepted it not as a human word, but as it actually is, the word of God, which is indeed at work in you who believe.
- An ambassador presents the case or the terms on behalf of the one who sent him
- Paul is saying that he is not just speaking on Christ's behalf, but it is as if Christ is speaking through him

5:21

- This verse is an explanation of how God can make reconciliation happen and what it means that God does not count our sin against us
- This is the most comprehensive summary of the Gospel
- Paul says that God made Him who had no sin to become sin for us
- We have to understand that this great verse of salvation must be first understood by the fact that we are lost

- We are lost in the mind of God as a result of our sin
- We are lost whether or not we feel lost
- We are lost because God says we are lost
- The Bible makes clear that we have offended a holy God
- The wrath of God must catch up with every person at some point
- His wrath can catch up with us at the cross or at the judgment
- The one who had no sin speaks of Jesus
- Notice first that this is something that God did
- Ultimately we can say that it was God who put Jesus to death
- Isaiah says it was God's will to crush Jesus
    - **Isaiah 53:10** - Yet it was the Lord's will to crush him and cause him to suffer, and though the Lord makes his life an offering for sin, he will see his offspring and prolong his days, and the will of the Lord will prosper in his hand.
- In Romans, Paul said that God displayed Jesus
    - **Romans 3:25** - [25] whom God displayed publicly as a propitiation [o]in His blood through faith. *This was* to demonstrate His righteousness, because in the forbearance of God He passed over the sins previously committed
- The love of Jesus is a demonstration of the love of God
    - **Romans 5:8** - [8] But God demonstrates His own love toward us, in that while we were yet sinners, Christ died for us.
    - **1 John 4:10- -** [10] In this is love, not that we loved God, but that He loved us and sent His Son *to be* the propitiation for our sins.
- Paul says that God sent His Son
    - **Romans 8:3** - [3] For what the Law could not do, weak as it was through the flesh, God *did*: sending His own Son in the likeness of sinful flesh and *as an offering* for sin, He condemned sin in the flesh,
- Jesus made clear he was not just a victim on the cross
    - **John 10:18** - [18] No one has taken it away from Me, but I lay it down on My own initiative. I have authority to lay it down, and I have authority to take

it up again. This commandment I received from My Father."

- Jesus was not crucified by the will of man
- Jesus was not crucified by the plan of Satan
- Jesus was crucified by the will and plan of God
- The question that we have to ask is when and where did God do this?
- When God looked at the cross, He chose to see Jesus as our sin
- Jesus was sin for us because God chose to view Him that way
- In other words, God made Jesus become sin in His own mind
- God imputed or accounted our sin to be on Jesus on the cross so that our penalty could be paid by Him in the mind of God
- This does not say that Jesus became sinful, it says he was made sin
- This also does not say that we were made righteous, it says we were made "the righteousness of God"
- The idea is that in the mind of God, our sin was credited to Jesus on the cross in that on the cross he paid the penalty for our lawbreaking
- So, what is it that Jesus became in the mind of God?
- He became the one that bore the penalty for our sin
- Jesus became sin for us only in God's mind and on the cross
- God, when He looked at the cross, which was planned by Him, chose to see the death of Jesus as our own sin
- What is it that we become in the mind of God?
- We become the righteousness of God in that God credits Jesus' dying to our accounts
- It is something that is credited or imputed to us
- That which is imputed is that which is spoken
- This arrangement is true because God has said it was true
- Our righteousness is imputed to us because God said so
- This imputing of righteousness and the making of Jesus to be sin is something that takes place in the mind of God
- When the Bible speaks about righteousness being imputed or credited to us, it means that this change happens in the mind of God and we only know it happened because God said it did
- God paid the ransom for our sin to Himself on the cross

- ○ **Hebrews 9:11-14** - [11] But when Christ appeared *as* a high priest of the good things to come, *He entered* through the greater and more perfect tabernacle, not made with hands, that is to say, not of this creation; [12] and not through the blood of goats and calves, but through His own blood, He entered the holy place once for all, having obtained eternal redemption. [13] For if the blood of goats and bulls and the ashes of a heifer sprinkling those who have been defiled sanctify for the cleansing of the flesh, [14] how much more will the blood of Christ, who through the eternal Spirit offered Himself without blemish to God, cleanse your conscience from dead works to serve the living God?
- The idea is of Jesus offering to God the fact of His death and God accepted it
- The offended God provided both the plan and the man for our salvation
- This verse explains that God has made the cross an arrangement with Himself for the forgiveness of our sins
- We might more specifically say that the cross is an arrangement set up by God between His love and His wrath
- Paul says that God created this arrangement so that we might become the righteousness of God
- The Bible makes clear that there isn't going to be anyone in Heaven who is not as righteous as God is
- This righteousness is an imputed righteousness which is found in Christ
- Notice, we are the righteousness of God "in Him"
- We do not become righteous in ourselves
- We are declared righteous by God
  - ○ **Romans 4:22-24** - [22] Therefore it was also credited to him as righteousness. [23] Now not for his sake only was it written that it was credited to him, [24] but for our sake also, to whom it will be credited, as those who believe in Him who raised Jesus our Lord

from the dead
- We are the righteousness of God in the mind of God
- In the book of Philemon, Paul asks Philemon to impute any wrong caused by Onesimus to his account
    - **Philemon 1:17-18 -** [17] If then you regard me a partner, accept him as *you would* me. [18] But if he has wronged you in any way or owes you anything, charge that to my account
- Where was Paul asking for this change of thinking to occur? He was asking for it to occur in the mind of Philemon
- The Bible talks about righteousness in two ways
- One way is the word justification which speaks of being forgiven
- The second way is the word sanctification which speaks of being changed into the likeness of Jesus
- Justification speaks of what God did for us
- Sanctification speaks of what God does in us
- We are not saved by what God does in us
- Roger Chambers says, "we are saved by what God has done outside of us, for us, because of us and in spite of us….we are saved by the cross."
- If we confuse sanctification with justification we can never have confidence in our salvation or assurance
- While our sanctification may go up and down, our justification is absolute as long as we are in Christ
- Verse 17 certainly speaks of a changed life, but we are not saved by a changed life, we are saved by the cross

2 Corinthians 6

- The phrase "working together with Him" speaks of being God's co-workers
- Paul had already stated that God had given him a ministry of reconciliation and called him to be an ambassador of Christ
- He is working together with God, as His ambassador to spread the message of reconciliation to the world
- Notice that Paul is working together with God, meaning that it is God's work, not his
- He implores the church not to receive God's grace in vain
- The idea is that they have received and accepted the grace of God
- What would it take for the Corinthians to get to the point where God's grace would have been received in vain?
- Receiving God's grace in vain would mean that they were not faithful to the end
- It is the idea of claiming to receive God's favor, but turning around and not living a transformed life
- It is equating the starting line with the finish line
- Perhaps he has in mind the Corinthians embracing some type of false teaching
- Perhaps he has in mind the Corinthians not living a life consistent with having been converted (5:17)
- Perhaps he has in mind them believing in a cheap grace which costs nothing
- Perhaps he has in mind a grace which still lives under the law and teachings of men i.e. Judaizers

6:2

- This is a quote from Isaiah 49:8
- This was a messianic prophecy about the coming of Jesus and the start of the New Testament dispensation
- Isaiah's words were directed to exiles in Babylon

- The idea was that something better than a return from captivity in Babylon was coming
- The phrase "acceptable time" means the time of God's favor
- Although we often use this statement, "today is the day of salvation" to speak to unbelievers making a decision to become followers of Christ, Paul directed it to believers
- Paul's message is that they are now living in the New Covenant dispensation where one can be reconciled to God through Christ
- It seems to be that the focus here is not on lost people accepting the Gospel, but on saved people having a sense of urgency in living our and sharing the Gospel

6:3

- When Paul says, "giving no cause for offense" he means that he has not done anything that should discredit his ministry or to view the Gospel in negative light
- He literally says, "placing an obstacle in front of no one"
- In other words, if people have rejected God's grace or received it in vain, it is not because of some defect in his character or witness
- His primary concern seems to be his ministry which is a ministry of reconciliation
- This does not mean that he dumbed down his preaching to avoid offending someone
- It means that no one could point to a problem with his character as their legitimate obstacle to coming to Christ
- People may have attempted to discredit Paul's ministry by worldly standards, but it would not be because of some error he made

6:4-5

- Paul does speak now of commending himself
- This at first sounds like a contradiction of what he said in 5:12
- It is as a servant of God that he commends himself
- However, it is not worldly criteria that he uses, but rather his

character and faithfulness to the Gospel
- He first speaks of his endurance
- Endurance is the virtue which is foundational to the other hardships that he will list
- In fact, he will list nine hardships that he has undergone
- Endurance is also connected to what he said about commending himself
- He commends himself as a servant of God with much endurance
- These nine things seem to fall into three categories of three

GENERAL HARDSHIP	SUFFERING CAUSED BY OTHERS	SELF-DISCIPLINE
Afflictions	Beatings	Labors
Hardships	Imprisonments	Sleeplessness
Distresses	Tumults	Hunger

- The first thing he mentions is afflictions
  - Notice that this word and the following are in the plural which indicates that they are not one-time events
- The second thing he speaks of is hardships
- The third thing he mentions is distresses
  - The word here means "in a narrow space"
- The fourth thing is beatings
  - The switch here is to suffering that was caused by other people
  - He will also speak of some of these in 2 Corinthians 11
  - He will state that he received a beating of 39 lashes on five occasions
  - Furthermore, he was beaten with rods on three occasions
- The fifth thing he speaks of is imprisonments
- The sixth thing is tumults
  - This speaks of riots
    - **Acts 13:50** - [50] But the Jews incited the devout women of prominence and the

leading men of the city, and instigated a
persecution against Paul and Barnabas,
and drove them out of their district.
- A disturbance broke out in Philippi due to his preaching
    - **Acts 16:19** - [19] But when her masters saw that their hope of profit was [i]gone, they seized Paul and Silas and dragged them into the market place before the authorities
- A riot started in Ephesus due to his preaching
    - **Acts 19:29** - [29] The city was filled with the confusion, and they rushed [s]with one accord into the theater, dragging along Gaius and Aristarchus, Paul's traveling companions from Macedonia.
- The Jews mobbed Paul in Corinth
    - **Acts 18:12-13** - [12] But while Gallio was proconsul of Achaia, the Jews with one accord rose up against Paul and brought him before the judgment seat, [13] saying, "This man persuades men to worship God contrary to the law."
- The seventh thing is labors
  - This is the first of the self-imposed hardships
  - Perhaps he has in mind taking a job as a tentmaker
- The eighth thing is sleeplessness
- The ninth thing he refers to is hunger

6:6

- Here, Paul's list shifts from hardships to moral qualities
- He will list six character qualities that he says govern his and the apostles' ministry
- First, he speaks of purity
  - This is referring to moral integrity
  - Perhaps there is even an idea of sexual purity and integrity

- Second, he says that they have knowledge
- Third, he says that they have patience
    - This is longsuffering or enduring difficult circumstances
- Fourth, he says that they have kindness
    - Kindness along with patience speaks of how we respond to abuse
- Fifth, he speaks of having a holy spirit
    - Many versions capitalize this and put a definite article in front of this to make it a reference to the Holy Spirit
    - However, it seems out of place to in the middle of these character qualification to make a reference to the presence of the Holy Spirit
    - There is no doubt that the apostles' ministry was marked by the help and activity of the Holy Spirit
    - Here, he is speaking of the fact that their character is holy
    - Paul used the same phrase in 1 Thessalonians 1, clearly speaking of his holy conduct
        - **1 Thessalonians 1:4-5 -**
          [4] knowing, brethren beloved by God, *His* choice of you; [5] for our gospel did not come to you in word only, but also in power and in the Holy Spirit and with full conviction; just as you know what kind of men we proved to be among you for your sake.
    - If we interpreted this to be a reference to the Holy Spirit, we would have to assume that with this Paul is shifting to a group which is speaking of the foundations of his ministry
- Sixth, he speaks about having genuine love
    - The word "genuine" means "without hypocrisy"
    - Paul is implying that some people act in a love that is not genuine

- Now, Paul will list three things which are foundations for his ministry
- These things point to the power that he relies on to accomplish his task
- First, he speaks of the Word of truth
    - This speaks of the fact that he was constantly speaking the truth
    - This was a common expression used to refer to preaching
    - Paul used this same phrase other places to speak of preaching
        - **Ephesians 1:13 -** [13] In Him, you also, after listening to the message of truth, the gospel of your salvation—having also believed, you were sealed in Him with the Holy Spirit of promise,
        - **Colossians 1:5 -** [5] because of the hope laid up for you in heaven, of which you previously heard in the word of truth, the gospel
        - **2 Timothy 2:15 -** [15] Be diligent to present yourself approved to God as a workman who does not need to be ashamed, accurately handling the word of truth.
- Second, he points to the power of God
    - This could speak of the power of the Gospel
        - **Romans 1:16 -** [16] For I am not ashamed of the gospel, for it is the power of God for salvation to everyone who believes, to the Jew first and also to the Greek.
    - Paul spoke of the Gospel having power
        - **1 Corinthians 2:4-5 -** [4] and my message and my preaching were not in persuasive words of wisdom, but in demonstration of the Spirit and of power, [5] so that your

faith would not rest on the wisdom of
men, but on the power of God.

- o This also could speak of the power of the Holy Spirit
  on display through miracles and signs
- Third, he refers to the weapons of righteousness
  - o There is some question as to whether he is speaking
    "weapons consisting of righteousness", righteous
    weapons or weapons provided by righteousness
  - o The difference may not be great either way
  - o If we interpret this to be weapons consisting of
    righteousness it would mean that he is speaking of
    godly character
  - o Certainly, a righteous character has great power
    when connected with the Gospel, even more so than
    deceitfulness
  - o If we interpret this to be righteous weapons then it
    may refer to the Word of God
  - o In Ephesians, when Paul spoke of the armor of God,
    the weapon that was spoken of was the sword of the
    Spirit which is the Word of God
  - o If we refer to this as weapons provided by
    righteousness then the idea is that it is speaking of
    God's imputed righteousness
  - o We certainly see the image of a spiritual battle and
    the apostles being equipped for it

6:8-10

- Now, he lists nine sets of contrasting responses to his work
- These all seem like paradoxes
- One lists the critical view of his work, the other lists the spiritual
  view of his work
- When we read this, we are reminded of the difficulty he faced as
  a servant of God
- Sometimes doing God's work means great difficulty and
  opposition, however, the heavenly reality makes the temporary
  difficulties worth it

- First, he says that he is received with both glory and dishonor
    - Surely Paul had moments of glory and dishonor. In other words sometimes Paul was valued and other times he was not

- Second, he says that he has been received with both evil report and good report
    - He literally says in defamation and in being well spoken of
    - The word translated "good report" is a word with which we get our word euphemism (*euphémia*) and it can mean commendation or praise
    - I am sure that there are times that good reports and bad reports were spread about Paul
    - There were also times he received good reports back from churches and time he received bad
    - Perhaps Paul would have drawn off of Jesus' words about how he was received
        - **Luke 6:26** - [26] Woe *to you* when all men speak well of you, for their fathers used to treat the false prophets in the same way.
- Third, he said that at times he is regarded as deceivers and yet at other times regarded as true
    - The idea of a deceiver is of a fake or an imposter
    - Deceiver is the word we get our word planet from; it literally carries the idea of one who causes others to stray
    - Paul's actions were always genuine and not from secret motives
    - It is clear that his critics may have claimed that he was not a true apostle

- Fourth, he says that he was unknown yet well known
    - There were times Christian people did not acknowledge him, welcome him or accept him
    - Some regarded him as a mere nobody with no authority

- o There we obviously others who regarded Paul quite highly
- Fifth, he says as dying yet we live
    - o He knew he was literally dying as he spoke of earlier, but yet he isn't defeated
    - o This is not just that he has not yet been put to death, but that he has not been beaten to the point that he has lost his desire to carry out his mission
    - o It is likely that here and in the next statement he has in mind the words of Psalm 118
        - **Psalm 118:17** - I will not die, but live, And tell of the works of the Lord.

- Sixth, he says he has been punished but not yet put to death
    - o His enemies haven't killed him…yet
    - o The word punished means "disciplined" or "chastened"
        - **Psalm 118:18** - The Lord has disciplined me severely,
            But He has not given me over to death.
- Seventh, he says that he is sorrowful yet always rejoicing
    - o At first, this seems to be a contradiction
    - o There may be several reasons that Paul was sorrowful
    - o He may have been sorrowful over his personal hardships
    - o He may have been sorrowful over being rejected by some brethren
    - o He may have been sorrowful over sin and false teaching
    - o He faced sorrow from circumstances, but maintained joy
    - o From jail, he was able to instruct the Philippians to "rejoice in the Lord always"

- Eighth, he says that he is poor yet making many rich
    - o This is a contrast between being earthy poor and

heavenly rich
- His commitment to Christ resulted in physical poverty
- They were made rich in Christ
- We are rich in Christ spiritually
- Paul's focus here is not on his personal richness, but on what he is giving away
- He is saying that his ministry and preaching is causing others to be spiritually rich
- He is physically poor. Spiritually rich. And he is giving away what he is rich in.
- Ninth, he says he has nothing yet possessing all things
  - Paul could have nothing yet have joy because his hope was not in things. He was not worldly minded
  - He possessed what really mattered
  - He willingly gave up his possessions
    - **Philippians 3:7-8** - [7] But whatever things were gain to me, those things I have counted as loss for the sake of Christ. [8] More than that, I count all things to be loss in view of the surpassing value of knowing Christ Jesus my Lord, for whom I have suffered the loss of all things, and count them but rubbish so that I may gain Christ

2 Corinthians 6 and the Beatitudes	
In afflictions, hardships and distresses, in beatings, in imprisonments and in tumults (6:4-5)	Blessed are those who have been persecuted for the sake of righteousness, for theirs is the kingdom of heaven (Matthew 5:10)
In purity (6:6)	Blessed are the pure in heart (Matthew 5:8)
In patience and in kindness (6:7)	Blessed are the meek (Matthew 5:5) Blessed are the merciful, for they shall receive mercy (Matthew 5:7)
By glory and dishonor, by evil report and good report; regarded as deceivers yet true (6:8)	Blessed are you when *people* insult you and persecute you, and falsely say all kinds of evil against you because of Me (Matthew 5:11)
In a holy spirit (6:6). By the weapons of righteousness (6:7)	Blessed are those who hunger and thirst for righteousness, for they shall be satisfied (Matthew 5:6)
Sorrowful, yet always rejoicing (6:10)	Blessed are those who mourn, for they shall be comforted (Matthew 5:4)
Poor, yet making many rich. As having nothing yet possessing all things (6:10)	Blessed are the poor in spirit, for theirs is the kingdom of heaven (Matthew 5:3)

6:11

- Here, Paul will describe two ways in which he and his companions have related to the Corinthians
- First, he says that their mouth has spoken freely
- Literally, this reads "our mouth has been opened to you"
- This Hebraic idiom means that they have spoken to them plainly
- The speaking plainly and frankly to them was motivated by a sincere love
- The addition of the phrase "O Corinthians" conveys a tenderness

and deep emotion
- Second, he says that they have "opened wide their hearts"
- The word "opened wide" comes from the Greek word *platuno* (πλατύνω) which means "enlarge" or "broaden"
- He means that he has opened up access to his heart to the Corinthians
- Paul means several things by this
- He means that the strain on their relationship was not caused by him
- Also, the use of the perfect tense means that he has not stopped loving them
- The making access available in his heart to the Corinthians would also make Paul vulnerable to the Corinthians

6:12

- The word "restrained" here connects back to the idea of their hearts being expanded or opened
- The restraining is the opposite of opening wide
- In other words, Paul is saying that the tension in the relationship is not because his heart is closed to them
- He says that they are restrained in their own affections
- That is the feeling of an open heart is not mutual
- In order for any relationship to thrive there has a be a mutual opening of the heart
- Paul is saying that he is open hearted to them, but they are narrow hearted towards him
- The word affections is the Greek word *splagchnon* (σπλάγχνα) which speaks of the inward parts or the bowels
- The bowels were viewed as being the seat of emotion and compassion
    - **1 John 3:17** - [7] But whoever has the world's goods, and sees his brother in need and closes his heart (*bowels*) against him, how does the love of God abide in him?

6:13

- The phrase "in a like exchange" means as a fair return for the kind of love he has shown to them
- Normally it would be strange to ask for a payback for a benefit received
- Paul's love for them was not condition. It was not a *quid pro quo*
- The first century philosopher Seneca wrote, "it is not easy to say whether it is more shameful to repudiate a benefit or to ask the repayment of it."
- Paul asks for repayment of his affection based on the fact that he is their spiritual father and they are his spiritual children
- He does not speak to them like they are childish, he speaks to them with the same affection that a father may speak to his children
- Sometimes a Father has to give loving correction to his children
- Paul has every right to expect his children to love him in return

6:14

- Now, Paul gives a strong admonition to the church
- He urges them to not be bound together with unbelievers
- The word "bound together" is the Greek word *heterozugeó* (ἑτεροζυγέω)
- This comes from two Greek words. One is the word *héteros* which means "another of a different kind". The other is the word *zygós* which means, "a yoke or joining two onto a single plow"
- So the idea is different kinds of people joined together but unevenly matched
- This is why sometimes the translation is "unequally yoked"
- In the book of Leviticus, in the LXX, the word is used to warn against mating two different types of animals
    - **Leviticus 19:19** - [19] 'You are to keep My statutes. You shall not breed together two kinds (*heterozugeó*) of your cattle; you shall not sow your field with two kinds of seed, nor wear a garment upon you of two kinds of material mixed together.

- Several questions emerge from this passage…
- First, who is the unbeliever that Paul has in mind?
- The word "unbeliever" here is a reference to non-Christian people
- The idea is of some connection a believer might make with someone who does not have the same spiritual background
- It is the idea of harnessing yourself to someone you are not spiritually compatible with
- In the book of Deuteronomy it was forbidden to yoke an ox and a donkey together
    - **Deuteronomy 22:10** - [10] "You shall not plow with an ox and a donkey together
- Second, what exactly is Paul prohibiting?
- We are not sure if there is a specific thing in mind to which Paul is speaking
- The Greek makes it clear that this is a prohibition of an action currently taking place
- Often times this is applied to the marriage relationship, but this is not just a prohibition of a Christian marrying a non-Christian
- Paul would not be suggesting that a believer has no interaction with an unbeliever
    - **1 Corinthians 5:9-11** - I wrote you in my letter not to associate with immoral people; [10] I *did* not at all *mean* with the immoral people of this world, or with the covetous and swindlers, or with idolaters, for then you would have to go out of the world. [11] But [f]actually, I wrote to you not to associate [g]with any so-called brother if he is an immoral person, or covetous, or an idolater, or a reviler, or a drunkard, or a swindler—not even to eat with such a one.
- Paul would not advocate a believer divorce an unbelieving spouse
    - **1 Corinthians 7:10-14** - [10] But to the married I give instructions, not I, but the Lord, that the wife should not leave her husband [11] (but if she does leave, she must remain unmarried, or else be reconciled to her

husband), and that the husband should not divorce his wife. [12] But to the rest I say, not the Lord, that if any brother has a wife who is an unbeliever, and she consents to live with him, he must not divorce her. [13] And a woman who has an unbelieving husband, and he consents to live with her, she must not send her husband away. [14] For the unbelieving husband is sanctified through his wife, and the unbelieving wife is sanctified through her believing husband; for otherwise your children are unclean, but now they are holy.

- It would make sense if the reference was to eating meat which had been offered to idols in the pagan temples
- Or maybe it speaks of a general partnership with unbelievers including marriage and business relationships
- I believe that the idea that Paul is conveying is that they have closed their heart to him, their spiritual father, and opened their heart to unbelievers
- This is a call for the believers to stick with him rather than to stick together with unbelievers
- It is likely that the Corinthians were being warned about forming their deepest and most meaningful alliances with unbelievers
- Paul will pose five rhetorical questions to make his point
- The assumed answer to all of these questions is "none"
- The first question he poses is: what partnership have righteousness and lawlessness?
- The question itself makes clear the contradiction of sin and righteousness partnering together for something
- Sin and righteousness cannot partner together because they have altogether different goals
- The word "partnership" is closely related to the word fellowship
- It means a participation, a sharing of something in common, or a close relationship between two people
- The obvious point is that righteousness and lawlessness have nothing in common
- Righteousness and lawlessness are opposites
- It is clear that righteousness is intended to represent the

Christian and their aim and lawlessness represents the pagan
- In Romans, Paul contrasts lawlessness and righteousness
    - **Romans 6:19** - ¹⁹ I am speaking in human terms because of the weakness of your flesh. For just as you presented your members as slaves to impurity and to lawlessness, resulting in *further* lawlessness, so now present your members as slaves to righteousness, resulting in sanctification.
- It is not possible to pursue sin and righteousness at the same time
- The one who is pursuing righteousness is naturally drifting further and further away from lawlessness
- A person who desires righteousness but partners with lawlessness will be pulled towards lawlessness themselves
- Hebrews (quoting Psalm 45:7) contrasts righteousness and lawlessness as well
    - **Hebrews 1:9** - "You have loved righteousness and hated lawlessness;
      Therefore God, Your God, has anointed You With the oil of gladness above Your companions."
- The second question is: what fellowship has light and darkness?
- Once again, the answer is "none"
- The word "fellowship" means a mutual sharing
- Light and darkness cannot co-exist
- By their very nature light and darkness exclude one another
- Darkness always points to unbelief or life outside of Christ
- Light refers to living in the truth of the Gospel
- The contrast between light and darkness is a very common idea in the New Testament
    - **John 3:19** - ¹⁹ This is the judgment, that the Light has come into the world, and men loved the darkness rather than the Light, for their deeds were evil.
    - **1 Peter 2:9** - ⁹ But you are a chosen race, a royal priesthood, a holy nation, a people for *God's* own possession, so that you may proclaim the excellencies of Him who has called you out of darkness into His marvelous light

- o **Colossians 1:13** - [3]For He rescued us from the domain of darkness, and transferred us to the kingdom of His beloved Son,

6:15

- The third rhetorical question is: what harmony has Christ with Belial?
- The word harmony is the Greek word *sumphónésis* from where we derive our English word "symphony"
- The idea is of a mutual agreement
- The name "Belial" (or *Beliar*) is a Hebrew name that is not found anywhere else in the New Testament
- The word is not ever used in the Old Testament to refer to a person
- The word is used several times in the Old Testament as a description
  - o **1 Samuel 2:12** - [12]Now the sons of Eli were worthless (*belial*) men; they did not know the Lord
- Belial means "worthlessness" or "corrupt"
- Sometimes the KJV uses the word "belial" rather than translate it as "worthless"
  - o **Judges 20:13** - [13]Now therefore deliver us the men, the children of Belial, which are in Gibeah, that we may put them to death, and put away evil from Israel. But the children of Benjamin would not hearken to the voice of their brethren the children of Israel (KJV)
- In the intertestamental period among Jewish literature (Dead Sea scrolls), the name was used to refer to Satan
- The fourth question asked is "what does a believer have in common with an unbeliever?"
- This is very similar to what was already said in verse 14
- There are many things that believers and unbelievers do share in common
- We share a common culture, community, language and

humanity with unbelievers
- The word "in common" can also speak of "portion"
- The believer does not have faith in Christ in common with the unbeliever
- The believer does not have spiritual goals in common with the unbeliever
- The believer does not have a Biblical worldview in common with the unbeliever
- The believer does not have godly values in common with the unbeliever
- The believer does not have the kingdom in common with the unbeliever
- The believer does not have a hope in common with the unbeliever

6:16

- The fifth and final question is "what agreement has the temple of God with idols?"
- In this instance, Paul defines that we are the Temple of God
- We, as opposed to a building are the dwelling place of God
- Starting in the second half of this verse, Paul will cite a series of Old Testament Scriptures to prove his point about being bound together with unbelievers
- The texts that he quotes from seem to focus on Israel's return from their exile
- The overall point is about maintaining some type of special distinction as the people of God and the danger of influences which would diminish their values
- The first reference goes back to both Leviticus 26:11-12 and Ezekiel 37:27
- The point is that God dwells within His temple and that we are His temple
- Furthermore, the idea of Him being our God and us His people speaks of a special covenant relationship
- The point is that as Gods holy people, with whom He dwells, we should separate from idol worship altogether

- The phrase "I will be your God; you will be my people" could be referred to as the theme of the Bible
- As we will see in these Scriptures that are quoted His covenant relationship with mankind focuses on His presence among His people and a mutual relationship

6:17

- The second Scripture that Paul references is Isaiah 52:11
- In the context, the place that there are told to come out of is Babylon
- The Jews were permitted to leave Babylon by the decree of Cyrus
- They were called to leave Babylon, go back to Jerusalem, but not take back with them the idols that were in Babylonian culture
- Here, the idea is not about leaving a literal Babylon, but a spiritual Babylon
- Then, in this verse there appears to be a reference to Ezekiel 20:34 where he says, "I will welcome you"
- In Ezekiel the idea is of God purging and then removing idol worshippers
- It is a warning to the disobedient and a promise to the faithful
- The phrase "I will welcome you" was dependent upon their obedience

6:18

- The reference in verse 18 is to 2 Samuel 7:14
- In context, God is speaking to David through Nathan the prophet about David's successor; Solomon
- It is a promise that Solomon would build the temple of God and that God would be a father to Solomon
- Paul is drawing from this and promising God's protection and fatherly love to those who are now His children

2 Corinthians 7

7:1

- This chapter begins with making application to the Old Testament Scriptures just mentioned at the end of chapter 6
- Paul says, "since we have these promises…"
- The promises are the promises just referenced in the Old Testament Scriptures which were quoted
- The promises deal with restoration, being welcomed and treated as sons and daughters
- The mentioning of these promises very clearly points to the fact that these promises are conditional
- The presence of these promises is a motivation for our upholding our end of the deal
- The promises are in the context of a clear warning
- This reminds us of the words about the promises of God in chapter 1
    - **2 Corinthians 1:20 -** ²⁰ For as many as are the promises of God, in Him they are yes; therefore also through Him is our Amen to the glory of God through us.
- As a result of these conditional, future promises, Paul gives an admonition to moral purity
- He says that we should cleanse ourselves from things that defile
- This is a clear call to an intentional avoiding of certain things
- The word translated "defilement" speaks of some type of religious defilement that comes from sin
- In chapter 6, the Corinthians were reminded that they were the Temple of the Living God
- They certainly would have understood the Old Testament concept of a Temple being defiled by something unclean or unholy
- What is true of physical temples, is also true of Christians
- It is sin that can defile us
- He speaks specifically about two different types of defilement
- He speaks about the defilement of the flesh and of the spirit

- This speaks of the whole person
- It is a warning against both external and internal moral defilement
- The flesh may speak of the physical activity that we do
- The spirit may speak more of what we think in our mind or hearts or attitudes
  - **Matthew 15:19-20** - [19] For out of the heart come evil thoughts, murders, adulteries, fornications, thefts, false witness, slanders. [20] These are the things which defile the man; but to eat with unwashed hands does not defile the man."
- Sin such as idolatry has both an internal and an external spiritual effect
- He speaks even further about what they are to pursue
- The first half of the verse covers the negative side of our pursuit of holiness (cleanse from all defilement)
- The second half of the verse covers the positive side of our pursuit of holiness (perfecting holiness)
- Holiness is not just about avoiding bad, sinful, spiritually defiling things…it is also about pursuing the right things
- The word "perfecting" speaks of bringing to completion or bringing to an end goal
- The phrase "perfecting holiness" speaks of striving for perfect holiness
- Holiness is the ultimate goal of the Christian
- There is a sense in which God counts us as holy through imputed righteousness
- However, here the idea is of something that we strive and aim for in our own lives
- The idea of being holy consists of three major components: Separateness, purity and wholeness

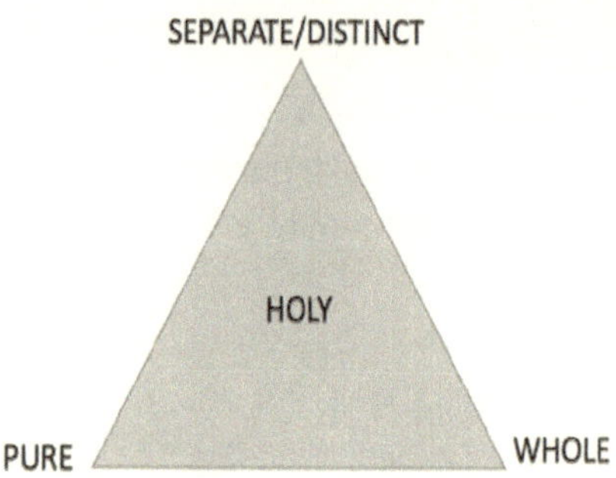

- o **Hebrews 7:26** - [26] For it was fitting for us to have such a high priest, holy, innocent, undefiled, separated from sinners and exalted above the heavens;

- The word "holy" means "set apart" or more literally "cut and separate"
- Paul's call here is for a moral purity that includes being separate from sin around them
- In 6:16, there was this specific call to "come out of her and be separate"
- The basis for this pursuit of holiness is the fear of the Lord
- This speaks of a reverence for God

7:2

- This is a repeat of his charge to the church that he gave in 6:13 where he said, "open wide to us also"
- He gives the Corinthians three defensive statements as to why they should make room for him in their hearts
- These statements say virtually the same thing
- They are all a defense of his personal character and actions towards them
- First, he says, "we have wronged no one"
- Second, he says, "we corrupted no one"
- Paul is saying that he did not corrupt any person either by means of their money or their teaching

- Third, he says, "we took advantage of no one"
- There is some question as to whether these are general defenses or specific defenses made due to specific accusations hurled at him
- Some have suggested that there was some type of accusation made about Paul's handling of the money that he was given
- I believe that it is more likely that it is a general defense of his character that may have touched on accusations made by some of his enemies
- In other words, Paul has not done anything to warrant personal animosity

7:3

- Paul claims that the intent of his defense is not to condemn them
- He means that by defending himself and proving that any accusation against him is unfounded that they should feel bad for their treatment of him, but he did not make the defense so that they would be shamed or guilted
- His defense of himself would naturally seem like a personal rebuke, however, the primary purpose was defending himself against unwarranted accusations
- Dying and living together speaks of a condition of friendship that exists in their hearts
- To live or die together means that in his mind they have a strong bond that cannot be broken
- He is saying that he is bound to them forever
- It seems interesting that in the order here, he talks about dying together prior to living together
- Perhaps he has in mind not just earthly life, but eternal life
- Thus, he would be saying, "look, we are going to spend eternity living together, it does not make any sense for us to be alienated now"

7:4

- This verse serves as a bridge between two sections of the letter

- Paul declares that he has "great confidence" in the Corinthians
- His confidence is that they will respond to his appeal by opening wide their hearts to him
- Second, he says that he "boasts on their behalf"
- This is a way of saying, "I have pride in you"
- While Paul will not make personal boasts, he does boast of his spiritual children
- This is the picture of a father being proud of his children
- Next, he makes clear that in the face of affliction he has reason for great comfort and joy
- This response seems to be in wake of news that he received from Titus about the church at Corinth

7:5

- Verse 5 will speak of the affliction he faced which he had made a brief mention of in verse 4
- We do not know the specific details about his time in Macedonia, but mentions a few details
- We know that Paul left Ephesus for Troas and from there he went in to Macedonia
- First, he speaks about the fact that they did not have a chance for rest when they came into Macedonia
- He did not have time for rest because he was busy with the work of the Lord
- Next, he says that he was afflicted on every side
- He faced affliction every place he went
- He faced affliction from within the church and outside the church
- It appears that the afflictions he faced were internal and external
- He describes them as "conflicts without and fears within"
- Whatever external difficulties he faced, caused internal turmoil
- Perhaps there were fears over persecution and opposition
- Perhaps there were fears over the future of the churches and specifically for the news from Titus
- Perhaps there were fears that his enemies would harm his reputation

- This gives some clarity to the nature of the comfort and joy he received in the midst of affliction
- Paul states that God gives comfort to the depressed
- The word the NASB translates as "depressed" is the Greek word *tapeinos* (ταπεινός) which can mean "down cast or humble. It has the idea of relying on God and not on self. The idea here is of being downcast.
- Paul is making clear that he was in need of some level of comfort
- It is likely that the truth that Paul echoes here comes from Isaiah 49:13
    - **Isaiah 49:13** - Shout for joy, O heavens! And rejoice, O earth! Break forth into joyful shouting, O mountains! For the Lord has comforted His people And will have compassion on His afflicted.
- It is interesting that Paul concludes that God provided the comfort he needed by the arrival of Titus
- Sometimes the comfort that God provides to us in our moment of need is through other people
- Paul was intending to meet up with Titus at Troas, but went on to Macedonia without him
- In 2 Corinthians 2, Paul spoke about his meeting up with Titus
    - **2 Corinthians 2:12-13** - [12] Now when I came to Troas for the gospel of Christ and when a door was opened for me in the Lord, [13] I had no rest for my spirit, not finding Titus my brother; but taking my leave of them, I went on to Macedonia.
- In chapter 2, Paul did not finish the account of not finding Titus
- The coming of Titus brought a great deal of comfort to Paul

- Here, Paul describes even more about the level of comfort that Titus' coming brought to him
- He was certainly somewhat comforted simply by the fact that he

finally met up with Titus
- However, Paul describes that there is more depth to the comfort that just a reunion
- He first of all was comforted himself by the comfort Titus received from the Corinthians
- This implies that the condition in the church seemed to be improving
- The Corinthians obviously had been impacted by Titus' stay and his teaching
- The condition of the church at Corinth brough comfort to Titus which in turn brought comfort to Paul
- Paul described part of the report that Titus brought to him for Corinth
- Titus conveyed three things that the Corinthian Christians felt towards Paul
- First, they had a longing
- This means that they longed for his return visit to them
- In the remainder of the letter, Paul will speak several times about a planned return visit
    - **12:14** - [14] Here for this third time I am ready to come to you, and I will not be a burden to you; for I do not seek what is yours, but you; for children are not responsible to save up for *their* parents, but parents for *their* children.
    - **13:1-2** - This is the third time I am coming to you. Every fact is to be confirmed by the [c]testimony of two or three witnesses. [2] I have previously said when present the second time, and though now absent I say in advance to those who have sinned in the past and to all the rest *as well*, that if I come again I will not spare *anyone*
- If they are longing for Paul's return, it implies that they have made whatever spiritual corrections might be expected in order to make the visit less painful
    - **12:20-21** - [20] For I am afraid that perhaps when I come I may find you to be not what I wish and may be found by you to be not what you wish; that

perhaps *there will be* strife, jealousy, angry
tempers, disputes, slanders, gossip, arrogance, disturb
am afraid that when I come again my God may
humiliate me before you, and I may mourn over
many of those who have sinned in the past and not
repented of the impurity, immorality and sensuality
which they have practiced.
  - **13:10** - [10] For this reason I am writing these things
    while absent, so that when present I *need* not
    use severity, in accordance with the authority which
    the Lord gave me for building up and not for tearing
    down
- Second, they had mourning
- This is the word *odurmos* (ὀδυρμός) which means sorrow or
  grieving
- This speaks of their sorrow and contrition over their past
  behavior towards Paul
- Perhaps their mourning is over their frustration with Paul for not
  at first planning to come to Corinth
- Third, they had a zeal
- They were not just okay with seeing Paul, they were zealous to
  see him again
- This all caused Paul to "rejoice more"
- The idea is that he rejoiced more than ever

7:8

- Paul speaks about the fact that his letter caused the church
  sorrow
- Sorrow was their initial response to his letter, not their final
  response
- The word "sorrow" will be a prominent concept in the remainder
  of this chapter
- The word for sorrow is the word *lupeo* (λυπέω) and can speak of
  a deep emotional pain or distress
- He acknowledges that the letter would have been a difficult
  thing to read

- He begins by telling them that he does not regret writing to them boldly even though it did cause sorrow
- Undoubtedly, Paul wrote a letter to the Corinthians in between first and second Corinthians dubbed the "painful letter" which is now lost
- This "painful letter" caused the church some level of sorrow
- It would seem that Paul's words hurt them to the core
- The result of this letter brought Paul himself mixed feelings
- On one hand he does not regret what he wrote because the type of sorrow that it produced was necessary
- On the other hand, he must have regretted not only that it hurt the Corinthians but also that it put a temporary strain on their relationship
- It does not say that his letter caused them anger, it caused them sorrow
- Now, they very well may have been angry, but it seems that the response was more sorrowful than anger
- Paul did not know their full response to this until he met up with Titus and got a report from him
- I picture Paul in some ways second guessing his letter for a time, but then realizing that it was necessary
- We can certainly understand Paul's sentiment today
- Some people are reluctant to rebuke or speak hard truths because they do not want to hurt people's feelings
- However, in many cases, such as the Corinthians, it was appropriate to speak the truth in love
- The truth can be a very difficult thing to hear because we do not always like our sins or faults pointed out
- Despite the fact that a stern rebuke might cause some initial sorrow, for the godly person it should end in repentance
- No preacher should enjoy inflicting sorrow upon his hearers even if the truth needs to be spoken
- Paul's goal was never to inflict pain or sorrow, it was to bring them to repentance
- Paul also reveals that the sorrow that they experienced as a result of the letter was only a temporary sorrow which would give way to genuine repentance

- Also, while we may feel for the sentiments of the person receiving a rebuke, it is wrong to assume that the one giving the rebuke does not feel the stress and emotional burden of doing so
- I do not believe that a person should rebuke someone if they do not have a similar emotional roller coaster that Paul had
- It never should be viewed as a simple, enjoyable or an easy thing to bring even a necessary rebuke

7:9

- Paul now reveals the final feeling that this harsh letter brought to him
- He says that his current view towards the whole thing is "joy"
- With all that he now knows, he says, "I rejoice that it made you sorrowful"
- He does not rejoice at their sorrow, he rejoices at the end result
- He rejoices at their repentance
- While sorrow over sin is a difficult thing for a season, it is God's will that we have sorrow over personal sin
- It is not possible to get to the point of genuine repentance without experiencing sorrow for sin first

7:10

- The sorrow that a person should have according to the will of God does not stay sorrow
- Notice that Paul speaks about two different types of sorrow
- One type of a godly sorrow which produces repentance and leads to salvation
- David is another example of someone who had godly sorrow over sin (2 Samuel 12:13; Psalm 51)
- The second type of sorrow produces death
- Paul says that the sorrow of the world produces death
- Notice that the response of sorrow may be the same, but what that sorrow produces is different
- The result of the sorrow is largely determined by what we believe

- If we are seeking God, then sorrow does not stop at the point of sorrow
- Judas is a great example of worldly sorrow
    - **Matthew 27:3-5** - [3] Then when Judas, who had betrayed Him, saw that He had been condemned, he felt remorse and returned the thirty pieces of silver to the chief priests and elders, [4] saying, "I have sinned by betraying innocent blood." But they said, "What is that to us? See *to that* yourself!" [5] And he threw the pieces of silver into the temple sanctuary and departed; and he went away and hanged himself.
- Judas was aware that what he did was wrong. He was sorrowful and even regretful for what he did, however it ended in death
- He had a worldly sorrow for his sin
- He may have legitimately felt bad for what he did, but it did not lead him to repentance or salvation
- Regret of sin is not the same thing as repentance of sin
- Judas regretted his sin
- The word used to describe Judas' sentiment is the Greek word *metamelomai* (μεταμέλομαι) which means regret
- The word for repentance is the Greek word *metanoia* (μετάνοια) which speaks of a change of the mind, a change of the heart, a change of the will leading to a change of action
- Esau is another Biblical example of worldly sorrow
    - **Hebrews 12:16-17** - that *there be* no immoral or godless person like Esau, who sold his own birthright for a *single* meal. [17] For you know that even afterwards, when he desired to inherit the blessing, he was rejected, for he found no place for repentance, though he sought for it with tears.
- When a person becomes sorrowful for something that they have done and is without hope of redemption or without the understanding of grace and forgiveness, it can easily lead to death
- While it is the will of God that an awareness of sin brings about some type of sorrow, it is not the will of God for us to wallow in our sorrow

- Remorse does not equal repentance
- The purpose of real sorrow is to lead to a change of action

7:11

- Here, we have a second list of the results of Titus' visit among the Corinthians
- The list is actually the results of their godly sorrow
- John the Baptist called his listeners to produce fruits in keeping with repentance
  - **Matthew 3:8** - [8] Therefore bear fruit in keeping with repentance
- These are the fruits of repentance from the Corinthians
- Genuine repentance can be measured in the change of conduct
- These traits indicate an abrupt and decisive change of thought and action
- In this list, we will see that the Corinthians' repentance is seen by a total change of direction in how they looked at people and things
- There are seven things listed here that sprang from godly sorrow
- The first is that it produced an earnestness with them
- The word "earnestness" can speak of speed, enthusiasm or diligence
- Paul is saying that they have an eagerness and a strong desire to do the right thing
- The second result in them is vindication
- The word for vindication here is the Greek word *apologia* (ἀπολογία) which speaks of a reasoned defense
- It was an ancient legal term which spoke of a person giving their defense in court
- The idea is that they had a real desire to clear their name
- This does not mean that they were attempting to excuse or justify past behavior
- Paul is saying that there future actions were attempting to right their past wrongs
- Third, it invoked indignation
- Indignation is a feeling of righteous anger that they had

- We do not know who or where their anger was being directed
- Perhaps their anger was at themselves for the way that they treated Paul
- Perhaps their anger was directed at the person in the church who has wronged Paul
- Perhaps their anger was directed towards whoever the offender that Paul has in mind might be
- Fourth, we see that their godly sorrow resulted in fear (*phobos*)
- The fear may speak of a godly and respectful fear of Paul's role as an apostle
  - **1 Corinthians 4:21** - [21] What do you desire? Shall I come to you with a rod, or with love and a spirit of gentleness?
- The fear may also refer to a reverential fear of God that came as a result of their godly sorrow which lead them to repentance
- Fifth, Paul again speaks of the longing that the Corinthians have
- In verse 7, the longing spoke of a longing to see Paul
- It is possible that this once again speaks of their longing for a return visit from Paul, which would indicate a restored relationship
- The longing could also speak of their longing to do what is right
- Sixth, Paul speak of their zeal
- Paul does not tell us what their zeal is directed towards
- Their zeal may be for God or even for a strengthened bond with Paul
- It is more likely that the zeal speaks of a renewed spiritual fervor or an awakening from spiritual apathy
- Lastly, he speaks of their avenging of wrong
- We do know that part of the issue that Paul had with the Corinthians was that they were not willing to discipline open, high-handed sin within the church
  - **1 Corinthians 5:2** - [2] You have become arrogant and have not mourned instead, so that the one who had done this deed would be removed from your midst.
- While at one time they were marked by indifference towards sin, now we see a willingness to act

- This would mean that they were willing to execute church discipline
- The speaks of their renewed desire to see justice done
- Perhaps it was a desire to discipline and silence false teachers and Paul's opponents within the church
- The action is probably not against the immoral brother of 1 Corinthians 5, but rather Paul's opponents in the church
- Perhaps there were even personal wrongs that they had done that they realized they needed to make restitution for
- Paul expresses a level of satisfaction with the Corinthians at the end of this verse

7:12

- Paul once again mentions the writing of the painful letter
- Paul says, "I did not write for the sake of the offended or the offender"
- We do not know exactly who the offended or the offender refer to
- This does not mean that he did not write with the goal of the offender being dealt with
- This does not mean that he did not write with the goal of defending the offended
- This phrase is a comparison that points to the highest aim and end goal of his writing
- For example, in Hosea 6:6, it says, "I desire mercy, not sacrifice"
- This does not mean that God did not desire or require sacrifice at all, it means that his highest aim is mercy
- His greater purpose was the ultimate good of the church
- He says that the end goal was "your earnestness on our behalf might be made known to you"
- That is he wants them to be reminded of their love and devotion to Paul
- Notice the phrase "before God"
- The church had not been considering its actions before God
- The reason that Paul wrote the painful letter was to remind them

of their relationship with Paul
- It should have caused them to consider Paul as one who is sent by God

7:13

- The "for this" speaks of the earnestness the Corinthians have on Paul's behalf
- Paul says that this result being accomplished brought him a level of comfort
- And over top of the personal comfort he received, he found joy because of Titus
- Now, Paul is not just finding personal joy in Titus' well-being
- He finds joy in Titus' joy
- We should always be willing to rejoice with those who rejoice
- Paul explains that Titus' soul was refreshed by the Corinthians
- Perhaps Titus was not expecting the type of reception and response that he received
- The faithfulness and obedience of listeners is a great source of encouragement to a preacher

7:14

- Paul had obviously spoke well of the church at Corinth to Titus
- It seems strange that Paul would have spoken so highly of a church with this many issues
- Not only that, Titus was sent to deal with an emergency spiritual situation
- Despite all of that Paul found reason to boast about the church
- This may make clear that the real problem in the church was not the majority, but just a few people who were causing trouble
- Paul says that his boasting about them was not proven false
- Titus' experience in Corinth confirmed Paul's boasting
- Paul is thankful that he was not made to look foolish by speaking well of the Corinthians only for Titus to come away with an altogether different perception

- Titus must have conveyed a couple of specific sentiments about the church in Corinth
- First, he speaks about their obedience
- There is no doubt that the church had serious issues that needed to be corrected, but Titus must have told Paul that they were teachable
- In order to be obedient, one must have a humble spirit
- The thing that they must have obeyed was in dealing with this offender in the church who was causing problems
- The measure of a person (or a church) is not necessarily that they have it all figured out, but that they are willing to obey the truth as they come to learn it
- The measure of the church's commitment to God and to Paul was their willingness to obey his teaching
- Second, he speaks about the spirit in which they received him
- They received Titus in fear and in trembling
- The phrase "fear and trembling" is one Paul uses other places as well
    - **1 Corinthians 2:3** - [3] I was with you in weakness and in fear and in much trembling
    - **Ephesians 6:5** - [5] Slaves, be obedient to those who are your [a]masters according to the flesh, with fear and trembling, in the sincerity of your heart, as to Christ
    - **Philippians 2:12** - [12] So then, my beloved, just as you have always obeyed, not as in my presence only, but now much more in my absence, work out your salvation with fear and trembling
- This does not mean that they were afraid of Titus
- The idea is always that of the attitude we should have in the presence of God or His Word
- This speaks of their humble, reverent spirit that anxiously desires to do the right thing
- This does not seem to be the attitude that they had during Paul's intermediate visit, but it is how Titus described his encounter

with the Corinthians

7:16

- Paul's confidence is that they would continue to do the right thing and remain faithful to God
- It is the confidence that Paul has that they are on the right track that will lead him to the plea to an act of generosity

2 Corinthians 8

8:1

- In chapter 8, we see a switch to a focus on the issue of giving
- The giving that is in mind is a special collection for the brethren in Jerusalem
- This need in Jerusalem is presented as an opportunity to give
- It was an opportunity to participate in something bigger than themselves
- It is important to see that the needs within the Jerusalem church were great and real
- When we saw the church in Jerusalem in the book of Acts, we saw that they themselves had a spirit of generosity
    - **Acts 4:32-35** - [32] And the congregation of those who

> believed were of one heart and soul; and not one *of them* claimed that anything belonging to him was his own, but all things were common property to them. [33] And with great power the apostles were giving testimony to the resurrection of the Lord Jesus, and abundant grace was upon them all. [34] For there was not a needy person among them, for all who were owners of land or houses would sell them and bring the proceeds of the sales [35] and lay them at the apostles' feet, and they would be distributed to each as any had need.

- It is possible that they gave themselves into poverty
- On top of that, we know that the need arose due to a famine
- It is also important to recognize that when a real need arose within the church that the church relied on the church to meet its needs
- They did not rely upon unbelievers in their community
  - **3 John 1:7** - [7] For they went out for the sake of the Name, accepting nothing from the Gentiles.
- They did not rely upon the government
- They did not host a fundraiser
- They were supported by Christians in other parts of the world
- Paul's appeal to the Corinthians begins by speaking about the grace given to the Macedonian Christians
- He is setting forth the Macedonian churches as the example of generosity
- The Macedonian Christians would refer to churches in Philippi, Thessalonica and Berea
- In 1 Corinthians 16, we saw that the Corinthians were already aware of a collection and that the Galatian Christians were as well
- Paul will hold forth the Christians in Macedonia as an example for them to follow
- It is interesting that Paul uses the word "grace" to speak of giving
- Grace usually speaks of God's unmerited favor towards us
- The idea is that generosity is an opportunity given to us by God

- In addition, generosity is a display of the fact that God's saving grace is at work within us
- The word "grace" will appear 10 times in chapters 8 and 9
- There are ten different words used in the New Testament to refer to a collection

DIFFERENT WORDS FOR GIVING IN THE NEW TESTAMENT

GREEK WORD	ENGLISH TRANSLATION	SCRIPTURE REFERENCE
logeias (λογείας)	Collection	1 Corinthians 16:1-2
charis (χάρις)	Free gift, grace	2 Corinthians 8:4
koinonia (κοινωνία)	Fellowship, sharing, participation, contribution	Acts 2:42, 2 Corinthians 8:4, 2 Corinthians 9:13, Romans 15:26
diakonia (διακονία)	Ministry, service	2 Corinthians 8:4, 2 Corinthians 9:1, 2 Corinthians 9:12-13
hadrotés (άδρότης)	Abundance, lavish generosity, bounty	2 Corinthians 8:20
eulogia (εὐλογία)	Praise, blessing, gift	2 Corinthians 9:5
leitourgia (λειτουργία)	Service, public gift	2 Corinthians 9:12
eleémosuné (ἐλεημοσύνη)	Alms, charity	Acts 24:17, Acts 10:2
prosphora (προσφορά)	Offering, sacrifice	Acts 24:17
dóron (δῶρον)	Gifts, present	Luke 21:1-4, Matthew 8:4, Matthew 23:18-19, Matthew 2:11

8:2

- Paul will mention something about the condition of the churches in Macedonia as he speaks about their example of generosity
- He will point out some things about the status of the churches in Macedonia
- First, he says that their condition was one of being under

affliction

- We know that the Macedonians were acquainted with persecution
  - **Philippians 1:29**-30 - [9] For to you it has been granted for Christ's sake, not only to believe in Him, but also to suffer for His sake, [30] experiencing the same conflict which you saw in me, and now hear *to be* in me.
  - **1 Thessalonians 1:6** - [6] You also became imitators of us and of the Lord, having received the word in much tribulation with the joy of the Holy Spirit,
  - **1 Thessalonians 2:14** - [14] For you, brethren, became imitators of the churches of God in Christ Jesus that are in Judea, for you also endured the same sufferings at the hands of your own countrymen, even as they *did* from the Jews
- The translation of this is "a great ordeal of affliction"
- The word "ordeal" speaks of proven character
- So, the thing that Paul is trying to convey is that they faced "proven character as a result of their many afflictions"
- Second, he points out that they had great poverty
- A combination of civil wars, invasions, Roman occupation resulted in poverty in Macedionia
- The word that explains their poverty and is translated as "much" is the Greek word bathos (βάθος) which means "down to the depths" or "deep"
- Notice that he also says that despite their great poverty they had an abundance of joy
- We see an example of poor people giving to poor people
- The Biblical idea of joy is of something that exists in the Christian regardless of the circumstances
- The Macedonians had joy in spite of affliction and poverty
- The paradox of this whole description is that the poverty of the Christians overflowed into generosity
- If there was a people who could pass on giving due to their current circumstances it may be the Macedonians
- In fact, it they may seem like the type that would need help

rather than give help
- They did not find their circumstance exempted them from generosity
- When all of the circumstances surrounding the Macedonian church was added together, it overflowed into generosity
- The Macedonian formula was: affliction + poverty + joy = wealth of liberality (generosity)
- In this case, one positive virtue outvalued two negative circumstances to produce a positive result
- For this result to take place we have to consider that in their case, the value of their joy equaled more than the combined value of their affliction and poverty
- It seems that generosity is a natural expression of real joy
- Paul uses the word "abounded" twice in this verse
- The Macedonian's joy and generosity both abounded
- The word "abound" means "to exceed what is normal or expected"
- The wealth that the Macedonians had was not a material wealth, but a wealth of generosity
- The word "generosity" here means a "singleness of heart" or "simplicity"
- The church of the first century had a unity
- The message was clear: if the Macedonians can give, anyone can give

8:3

- Here we find two descriptions of the Macedonian giving
- First, they gave beyond their ability
- Paul suggests they did not just give what they were able to give, but they went over and beyond
- This is the picture of sacrificial giving
- Sometimes the existence of a real need demands not just giving, but sacrificial giving
- This is not a story of people prospering and then giving out of their surplus
- If the churches in Macedonia were poor, it is possible that the

actual amount that they collected was not much, but the way that
they gave was impressive
- The emphasis is not on the quantity of their giving, but on the
spirit in which they gave
- Their generosity reminds us of the widow's mite
    - **Luke 21:1-4** - And He looked up and saw the rich
      putting their gifts into the treasury. [2] And He saw a
      poor widow putting in two small copper coins. [3] And
      He said, "Truly I say to you, this poor widow put in
      more than all *of them*; [4] for they all out of
      their surplus put into the offering; but she out of her
      poverty put in all that she had to live on."
- Second, their giving was voluntary
- He says they gave of their "own accord"
- This literally means they gave with "self-choice"
- The Macedonians did not have to be asked or convinced to give
- Paul did not in any was coerce them to give

8:4

- A few things become evident from what Paul says here…
- First, the Macedonians actively sought out the chance to give
- It was not just that they were willing to give, but they were
looking for a chance to give
    - **Isaiah 32:8** - But a generous man devises generous
      things, And by generosity he shall stand (NKJV)
- It is not uncommon for someone to give if they are asked or
solicited, it is uncommon to plead for the chance to give
- Second, they had to plead with Paul to do this
- The word used for "plead" implies more than asking. It is closer
to begging.
- It is not often that a donor has to plead with the solicitor to give
- Perhaps Paul would have been reluctant to take money from
such a poverty stricken group
- At the very least, it appears that while Paul would ask the
Galatians and the Corinthians to join in this collection, that he
did not intend on asking the churches in Macedonia

- Third, they saw giving as a privilege not a burden
- Notice the use of the words "favor" and "participation" which Paul uses to describe their view of the collection
- The word "favor" is the same word as "grace"
- They wanted to participate in this collection
- The word "participation" here is the Greek word *koinonia* (κοινωνία) which means fellowship or a sharing
- Fourth, they viewed giving as a ministry
- The word translated "support" is the Greek word *diakonos* which speaks of service or ministry
- It carries the idea of supporting the needs of others
- There is a difference in the way we do something when we consider something we do as a ministry and a privilege
- The Macedonians must have been convinced that the need of the saints in Jerusalem was more important than them having some material goods
- When we see that there is an urgent need in the kingdom, we should view it as our ministry to meet it
- We may give to a good cause out of our overflow, but in order to give sacrificially we really have to believe in what we are giving to

8:5

- Paul suggests that the Macedonian Christians gave beyond what any reasonable expectation may have been
- This verse explains how they were able to give in the sacrificial way that they did
- He will point out their dedication to the Lord and their loyalty to him
- Paul says, "they gave themselves first to the Lord"
- This speaks of the Lord being first in their priorities
- Notice that the thing that the Macedonians first gave to God was not money it was their whole selves
- Once a person has given themselves to God, giving of money is an easy step
- Generosity flows from a devotion to the Lord

- Giving ourselves to the Lord means that we make ourselves and our resources available to God
- One reason that a lack of giving is a spiritual problem is because it is most likely a symptom of a much greater devotion problem
- The second order of priority was that they gave themselves to Paul
- When he says, "gave themselves to us" he means that they were in submission to him and in support of this specific work

8:6

- It seems that part of the reason for Titus' trip to Corinth was to urge them to continue in this venture of generosity to which they had at one time started
- This is an admonition that the Corinthians might fulfill their commitment to participate in this special collection
- Rather than blast the Corinthians, he cites their initial commitment as the target for them
- Sometimes we need to be exhorted and encouraged to finish good works that we began

8:7

- Paul calls on the Corinthians to "abound" in generosity
- The word translated "abound" was used in 8:2 to describe how the Macedonians poverty resulted in generosity
- To "abound" is to have more than enough of something
- In order to make this point, Paul says that they should have the same "over and beyond" mentality with giving that they have in other areas of their faith
- He will cite five areas of faith that the Corinthians always abound in
- The list here sounds similar to the statement he made in 1 Corinthians 1
    - **1 Corinthians 1:5** - [5] that in everything you were enriched in Him, in all speech and all knowledge

- This list falls into two categories
- The first three traits speak of spiritual gifts
- The second two traits speak of Christian virtues
- First, he says that they abound in faith
- This probably points to a spiritual gift that was present in the church through which they were able to perform miraculous gifts of the Spirit
    - **1 Corinthians 12:9** - [9] to another faith by the same Spirit, and to another gifts of healing by the one Spirit,
- Second, he says that they abound in utterance
- The word "utterance" is "speech"
- It probably has reference to the speaking in tongues
- Third, he says that they abound in knowledge
- This speaks of the spiritual gift of knowledge
    - **1 Corinthians 12:8** - [8] For to one is given the word of wisdom through the Spirit, and to another the word of knowledge according to the same Spirit;
    - **1 Corinthians 13:2** - [2] If I have *the gift of* prophecy, and know all mysteries and all knowledge; and if I have all faith, so as to remove mountains, but do not have love, I am nothing.
- While we do not have the spiritual gift of knowledge available to us today, we certainly should strive to abound in our knowledge of God and His Word
- However, knowledge should overflow into action
- Fourth, he says that they abound in earnestness
- This speaks of their eagerness to do what is right
- Paul is urging that they have the same eagerness to share in the collection as well
- Fifth, he says that they abound in love
- Real love should be displayed in their actions
- Paul is pointing out that for the Corinthians, they do abound in love already and this collection would fit in with that
- He urges the same type of attitude in "this gracious work"
- I do not believe that this means that they were hesitant to abound in the collection, but their commitment may have waned

- All of those other five traits that they abound in should lead
  them to abound in generosity
- They should seek to share in this collection with the same
  passion and diligence that they seek to excel at these other
  aspects of their faith
- Perhaps this verse is somewhat tongue in cheek
- The argument may be, "it's great that you have all these other
  things that you strive for and are good at, but maybe you should
  strive for generosity with the same passion that you do those
  things."

8:8

- As an apostle, Paul certainly could have given some type of
  command to the church that they participate in this giving
- I do not believe that because he is not commanding them that it
  means that he is indifferent to their response
- The truth is that there is only one adequate response for the
  church and that is to give generously
- He wants them to want to give
- He does not want them to give because they feel that they have
  to, he wants them to give because they get to
- Paul puts the opportunity to give as a test which is geared to
  prove the sincerity of their earnestness and their love for others
- In other words, if they for some reason elected not to abound in
  giving that it would be an indictment of a deeper spiritual issue
- Paul is suggesting that their actions should reflect their words

8:9

- Earlier, Paul set forth the example of the Macedonians for their
  sacrificial giving
- Now, he sets Jesus as an example of sacrificial giving
- Jesus' love compelled Him to give
    - **John 3:16** - [16] "For God so loved the world, that
      He gave His [e]only begotten Son, that
      whoever believes in Him shall not perish, but have

eternal life.

- Genuine love always leads to giving
- When he speaks of the "grace" of Jesus he is speaking of his favor towards us displayed through the gift of His sacrifice on the cross
- Some people would connect the talk of Christ exchanging riches for poverty as a statement about incarnation
- The Bible certainly speaks of Jesus giving up riches of glory to come to Earth
    - **Philippians 2:6-8** - [6] who, although He existed in the form of God, did not regard equality with God a thing to be grasped, [7] but emptied Himself, taking the form of a bond-servant, *and* being made in the likeness of men. [8] Being found in appearance as a man, He humbled Himself by becoming obedient to the point of death, even death on a cross.
- However, when Paul speaks of Jesus being "rich" he is not merely speaking of his position in Heaven
- This is not speaking not just of His incarnation, but also His death on the cross
- The focus is not on Jesus' life as a poor carpenter, but on the whole sacrifice that He made from leaving glory to come to Earth to dying on the cross
- Christ being "rich" brings out the idea that He was without sin
- It echoes a similar thought as 5:21, "God made Him who knew no sin to become sin for us"
- Christ becoming poor speaks of the fact that He paid the debt for our sin
- The point of this is that Jesus gave up what He had for the sake of someone else in a display of genuine love
- The riches of salvation are made available to us because of what Jesus gave

8:10

- Paul points out that the Corinthians were among the first who were on board for this special collection

- When they had initially decided to be a part of this collection, it was something that they desired to do
- We do not know what changed in this, but evidently their desire to give cooled

8:11

- Paul is urging them to complete what they started with the same eagerness
- It seems that the Corinthians wanted to give, but that desire to was not accompanied by action
- There is something to be said about completing something that you started and promised to do
- The phrase, "but finish doing it also" is the only imperative command in this chapter
- The statement "by your ability" means "out of what you have"
- Paul is not asking the Corinthians to do as the Macedonians and give beyond their ability, but to give out of what has been given to them
- The reality is that the Corinthians churches likely had more ability to give than the Macedonians churches did

8:12

- Their "readiness" speaks of their willingness and eagerness to give
- Paul says that the gift is "acceptable"
- The gift being acceptable speaks of how God views their gift
- God accepts a gift as honorable when it is given from a sincere desire to give
- It is not the amount that God is most concerned with, it is the willingness to give it
- Even a large gift would not be pleasing to God if it did not come from a sincere willingness to give, or if it was given begrudgingly
- He says, "not according to what he does not have"
- In other words, God does not hold us responsible to give what

we do not have
- However, He does expect generosity with what we have
- We can only give of what we have
- Not every person can give the same amount, but everyone can give something

8:13

- Paul points out that the purpose of this giving is not about easing the suffering of the saints in Jerusalem while creating poverty in Corinth
- The truth of the matter is that the giving may have created some real need among them
- Perhaps by saying this, Paul is answering some objections that the Corinthians may have been having
- Perhaps they would have been saying, "if we give to them to ease their affliction, we will then be poor and afflicted"
- Perhaps some would have questioned the logic of helping people that they did not know
- Perhaps some in Corinth did not think that it was fair that other people gained from what they worked for
- Do not forget that the idea of giving in this chapter is that it is a grace. It is not fair. It is merited. It is undeserved
- Paul speaks about the goal of equality
- The word that Paul uses for "equality" is the word "*isos*" from where we get the word isosceles
- It is very likely that Paul is not suggesting that every person should have absolutely equal financial wherewithal
- I do not believe that he is calling for an implementation of Acts 2:45 on a global scale
    - **Acts 2:45** - [45] and they *began* selling their property and possessions and were sharing them with all, as anyone might have need.
- What Paul has in mind is not that every person have

equal financial standing

- He is calling for "equity" not necessarily "equality"
- The word equity speaks of fairness or justice

> **Equity:**
> noun, plural eq·ui·ties.
> 1. the quality of being fair or impartial; fairness; impartiality: the equity of Solomon.
> 2. something that is fair and just: the equities of our criminal-*justice system.*

- In other words, the giving is not about leveling the

playing field, it is about doing what is right and fair

8:14

- We really see here more of what Paul meant by "equality"
- He was saying that it is only right that since they have an abundance that they help someone who lacks
- Paul describes the Corinthians as having "abundance"
- He was calling upon the Corinthians to give up their abundance to help those who had nothing
- He lets them know that if they are in need that they could expect someone somewhere who has abundance to give to them as well
- There may be times in life where we have an abundance. In those seasons we should be generous givers
- However, there may be a season of life where we are lacking and need to rely on the generosity of others
- Paul is supposing that if the saints in Jerusalem are going to accept a gift in their season of need that they should likewise be willing to give when they have an abundance
- This verse also may warn about the danger of hoarding wealth
  - **Proverbs 3:27-28** - Do not withhold good from those to whom it is due, When it is in your power to do *it*. [28] Do not say to your neighbor, "Go, and come back, And tomorrow I will give *it*," When you have it with you.
  - **Ecclesiastes 5:13** - [13] There is a grievous evil *which* I

have seen under the sun: riches being hoarded by their owner to his hurt
  - **James 5:1-3** - Come now, you rich, weep and howl for your miseries which are coming upon you. [2] Your riches have rotted and your garments have become moth-eaten. [3] Your gold and your silver have rusted; and their rust will be a witness against you and will consume your flesh like fire. It is in the last days that you have stored up your treasure!

8:15

- The Old Testament quotation here is taken from Exodus 16:18
- The context is in dealing with the collection of the manna in the wilderness
- The idea that was taught through the manna was that when gathering each family should take only what they need
- In fact, there was a warning about taking more than needed
- The point Paul is conveying is that we can give to others out of our abundance and still have enough for ourselves
- God's principle was that no one was to have too much and no one was to have too little
- In the illustration of the manna, Paul is conveying three truths to the Corinthians
- First, they have enough to share with others and still enough for their needs
- Second, the abundance can rot
  - **Exodus 16:18-21** - [18] When they measured it with an omer, he who had gathered much had no excess, and he who had gathered little had no lack; every man gathered as much as he should eat. [19] Moses said to them, "Let no man leave any of it until morning." [20] But they did not listen to Moses, and some left part of it until morning, and it bred worms and became foul; and Moses was angry with them. [21] They gathered it morning by morning, every man as much as he should eat; but when the sun

grew hot, it would melt.
- Third, God uses other people to supply our needs
- God was using the Corinthians to supply the needs of those in Jerusalem

8:16-17

- There is a brief shift here where Paul will speak about the ones that he has sent out to go to Corinth
- He speaks a little more about the sending of Titus
- When Paul says that Titus has the "same earnestness on your behalf" he means that Titus has the same feeling towards the Corinthians and this offering that Paul has
- Part of the reason that Titus was at Corinth was to encourage them regarding this specific offering
- Paul makes it very clear that Titus has a special concern about this specific project
- Paul wanted to pause and give thanks to God that Titus has this same passion for this cause

8:18

- We do not know who this brother is that Paul sent along with Titus
- Paul suggests that this person is well known for his gospel work
- Paul actually heralds his work "in the Gospel" meaning his work has to do with evangelismn
- Several ideas have been conveyed by different people
    - Luke
    - Barnabas
    - Silas
    - Mark
    - Timothy
    - Aristarchus
- Many people feel that the brother may have been one of the names mentioned in Acts 20 who were carrying the offering to Jerusalem or Luke, who wrote the book of Acts

- ○ **Acts 20:4** - ⁴ And he was accompanied by Sopater of Berea, *the son* of Pyrrhus, and by Aristarchus and Secundus of the Thessalonians, and Gaius of Derbe, and Timothy, and Tychicus and Trophimus of Asia.
- Luke has been a very common guess throughout history, but there is no evidence one way or another

8:19

- It appears as though the churches that were involved in contributing to this collection were involved in selecting a delegation to deliver it
- Paul speaks of two main goals of this whole collection
- First, Paul says that the goal of this gracious work was for the glory of the Lord
- It was not about the churches getting credit or praise, it was about bringing God glory
- The Bible certainly teaches that all things that are done should be done for the glory of God
- Second, he says that it was about showing their readiness to help when a need was present

8:20

- Paul implies that he was taking precautions so that no one could accuse him or others of any impropriety
- He has already experienced his character being maligned
- The first century world was full of deceivers who tricked people for money
- Paul wanted to make sure he went above and beyond to make sure no person could accuse him of mishandling such a collection
- When dealing with money there is always a great risk of a false accusation
- The representatives from these other churches could vouch for Paul and his companions integrity with the money
- Notice that Paul's concern was the someone might discredit him

- The word for "discredit" means to find fault or to slander
- Even if nothing wrong had taken place, he wanted to make sure that he left no room for someone to find fault in his handling of this offering
- The word for abundance here is the Greek word *hadrotes* (ἁδρότης) and it means "lavish or thickness"
- Paul's concern was not just for the protection of the offering or his reputation, but the cause of the Gospel
    - **1 Corinthians 9:12** - [12] If others share the right over you, do we not more? Nevertheless, we did not use this right, but we endure all things so that we will cause no hindrance to the gospel of Christ.

- We should constantly be mindful whether our actions could hurt the church, the Gospel or our witness for Christ

8:21

- This is a reference to Proverbs 3:4
- It is not enough that he just do right in the eyes of the Lord
- His actions and motives are clearly visible to God
- He had to make sure that he stayed above reproach in the eyes of man
- He did not want his ministry to be hurt by some hint of dishonesty
- How other people view our actions matters
    - **1 Thessalonians 5:22** - Abstain from all appearance of evil (KJV)
- Many Christian leaders have hurt the kingdom by mishandling money or dishonesty with funds
- Even when going to extra lengths to stay above reproach, people can criticize or attack what we do
- Jesus was aware that these things would happen as well
    - **Matthew 5:11** - [11] "Blessed are you when *people* insult you and persecute you, and falsely say all kinds of evil against you because of Me

- In spite of that, we should do the best we can to be above reproach in all things

8:22

- This appear to be another "brother" different from the one mentioned in verse 18
- This particular brother is said to have been "often tested"
- We do not know what testing this speaks of exactly
- In Greek the phrase "tested and found diligent" is one word which implies a test that has been passed
- For him to have been tested means that he has proven himself to be faithful in other responsibilities delegated to him
- Paul's point is that he is not just sending a novice in this delegation, but rather he is sending people who have proven themselves to be reliable and faithful over time

8:23

- Here, Paul commends both Titus and the two brothers mentioned above
- First, Paul speaks of Titus as being his partner and fellow worker in Corinth
- Paul is reminding them that Titus has worked hard for the Lord for the same cause that Paul worked for in Corinth
- He refers to the two brothers as "messengers of the churches"
- The word for messenger here is the Greek word *apostolon* (ἀπόστολος)
- They did not hold the office of apostle, but they were sent out from the church for a specific responsibility
- There is a difference between the office of apostle and an apostle (one who is sent) of the church
- Paul further described these brethren as a "glory to Christ"
- That is in their work for the Lord and the conduct of their character, they bring glory to Christ
- The construct here implies not only that they honor Christ, but rather that they reflect the character of Christ

- Paul asks the church at Corinth to show proof of their love for them
- This is Paul's appeal for the church to "put their money where their mouth is"
- There are several ways that the church can show proof of the love that they profess
- First, they can receive and accept this delegation with open arms
- Second, they can continue their participation in the collection for which they are involved
- Love is not something merely with words, but shown through deeds

2 Corinthians 9

- There are some commentators who suggest that chapter 9 was a separate letter altogether from 2 Corinthians
- Some say this was another letter sent to other churches in Achaia
- It is our view that this was not a separate letter from 2 Corinthians at all and fits the context of the letter

9:1

- Chapter 9 connect very nicely to chapter 8 by the phrase "for to begin with" or "for concerning now" (*peri men gar*) which in the NASB is simply translated as "for" (it is ignored completely in other translation such as the NIV)

-

> **Superfluous:**
> *adjective*
> 1. being more than is sufficient or required; excessive.
> 2. unnecessary or needless.

When he says it is "superfluous" for me to write to you, he means that it is unnecessary

- The phrase may sound a little

bit like a parent who says,
"I know I do not need to tell you this again, but…".

- Or maybe the phrase is akin to a preacher

saying, "in conclusion".

- Interestingly, chapter 9 begins by Paul saying that he does not need to write to them about this special ministry to the saints after he had just written to them about this special ministry to the saints in chapter 8. He then will talk about the collection for the remainder of chapter 9 as well
- Paul did not need to speak more about the offering for the saints because he has already said quite a bit about it (1 Corinthians 16:1-4)
- Paul did not need to speak any more about the offering for the saints because he was sending Titus to them with some more direction
- Paul did not need to speak any more about the offering for the saints because he had already been informed that they were back on track

9:2

- Just as he boasted to the Corinthians about the Macedonians, he also boasted to the Macedonians about the Corinthians
- The thing that he boasted about was their readiness to help

- He had already spoken of the fact that the Corinthians were ready and eager to give (8:11)
- From the initial plea in to join in the giving in 1 Corinthians 16, the Corinthians were on board
- Achaia speaks of the Roman province of which Corinth was the capital city
- Paul declares that the zeal of the Corinthians has effectively stirred up the Macedonians
- The word "stirred up" is the Greek word *erethizó* (ἐρεθίζω) can mean to stir up, provoke, incite or arouse
- The word can be a positive thing or a negative thing depending on the context (See Colossians 3:21 where the word is used negatively)
- Here, the "stirring up" was a positive thing
- The Corinthian's enthusiasm inspired the Macedonian giving
- Reports of faithfulness to God and good works can inspire others to do good works

9:3-4

- In chapter 8, Paul spoke about the sending of a team lead by Titus to Corinth
- Here, Paul wants to make sure that the Corinthians are prepared to pass on their collection that they have been preparing for
- He says that he does not want his boasting about them to prove "empty"
- The way Paul's boast about them would be made empty is for the delegation to arrive and the Corinthians not have anything to contribute
- Judging from Paul's words here, it is possible that there are some Christians from the region of Macedonia who are travelling to receive and then deliver this collection
- Paul does not want the Macedonian representative to get to Corinth and find that Paul's boasting about them was not an accurate depiction of the reality
- Paul connects his own personal honor with the Corinthians
- If this were to happen, Paul makes clear that both he and the

Corinthians would be embarrassed by this misplaced confidence
- Notice where the word "confidence" is spoken of at the end of verse 4. The word used is the Greek word *hypostasis* (ὑπόστασις) which means a "guaranteed arrangement". It speaks of a plan
- It is not just that Paul is concerned about his own honor if the Corinthians are unprepared to contribute, he is concerned about the whole collection being at risk

9:5

- Evidently, the Corinthians had already promised a contribution
- If the Corinthians failed to give a gift, they would then be promise breakers
- It is said that the names of pledge breakers were published in the *agora* (marketplace) in Athens
- While Paul does give the warning about breaking a pledge, this should not be the main motivation to give
- Paul uses the word for "bountiful gift" speaks of the offering
- The word for "bountiful gift" means it is a blessing
- Paul is urging them to give as a blessing not because of covetousness or greed
- This speaks of giving just to satisfy someone else's expectations
- This is a challenge to their motives
- Paul did not want them to give because they were being forced to, because they were worried about their reputation or because they were guilted into it
- Our motivation in giving matters more than the amount that we give

9:6

- In the next six verses, Paul will use four different lines of reasoning to further compel the Corinthians to give
- The first thing that Paul does is quote a proverb
- The proverb that Paul uses is a farming illustration
- The lesson is quite simple and obvious: the amount that a farmer

harvests corresponds to the amount that the sow
- For Paul, sowing correlates to their giving
- Now, Paul is not giving investment advice for material prosperity
- However, Paul will teach that God blesses generosity
- The word for "bountifully" is the same word that is used in verse 5 which could better mean "sows in blessings…will reap blessings"
- The point is not just about giving a large sum, but giving with the attitude of wanting to be a blessing and with an attitude of blessing God
- Paul does not reveal the exact nature of the blessings that the generous will reap
- Paul also does not reveal when those blessings will be claimed
    - **Galatians 6:9** - [9] Let us not lose heart in doing good, for in due time we will reap if we do not grow weary.

9:7

- This verse is one of the most cited verses about giving
- When the New Testament teaches on giving it does not, like the Old Testament, set a percentage amount such as the tithe
- Instead, the instruction is to "give whatever you decide"
- The amount to be given is something that has been "purposed in a person's heart"
- The idea is that giving should not be an impulse decision, but rather premeditated
- Paul refers to two attitudes that should not control the decision of giving
- First, he says that one should not give grudgingly
- The word used here speaks of "emotional pain" or grief
- Some versions translate this "reluctantly" but that might not quite capture the force of what is being said
- Second, he says that one should not give under compulsion
- A person should not give because they have been guilted or tricked into it

- Giving should be voluntary
- The second method that Paul uses to urge the Corinthians to give is to reference Scripture
- The idea conveyed in the Scriptures is that if a person gives reluctantly the benefit and blessing of giving is removed from that person
  - **Deuteronomy 15:10** - [10] You shall generously give to him, and your heart shall not be grieved when you give to him, because for this thing the Lord your God will bless you in all your work and in all your undertakings.
- Paul then tells the Corinthians that God loves a cheerful giver
- This is a quotation from the Septuagint version Proverbs 22:8 which says, "God blesses a cheerful and giving man"
- The word for "cheerful" is the Greek word Hilarion (ἱλαριόν)
- It is where we get our English word "hilarious"
- The point is that giving should make us filled with joy
- A 5th century theologian named Maximus of Turin wrote: "Joyful and cheerful then is one who attends to the poor. Quite clearly, he is joyful, because for a few small coins he acquires heavenly treasures for himself; on the contrary, the person who pays taxes is always sad and dejected. Rightly is he sad who is not drawn to payment by love but forced by fear. Christ's debtor then is joyful and Caesar's is sad, because love urges the one to payment and punishment constrains the other; the one is invited by rewards, the other compelled by penalties."[1]

9:8

- The third thing that Paul uses to urge the Corinthians to give is a reminder of God's provision
- He lifts up the fact that God is able to supply
- The grace that God makes abound to us here has to do with our physical needs being met
- The point is that God provides all that is needed for both themselves and in order to be generous
- This verse uses the repetition of the word "all" in order to

- emphasize the point
- In fact, the word all in some for is used five times in this verse
    - **All** grace
    - **Every** way
    - **Always**
    - **All** Sufficiency
    - **Every** good work
- The application that Paul is making is that if someone is not generous that it means that they do not trust that God will supply all that they need
- Paul says that we always have all sufficiency
- Our giving does not have be seasonal or depend on us hoping to get what we need. Paul says we always have what we need
- The word "having all you need" speaks of self-sufficiency or contentment
- All Sufficiency speaks of having adequate resources ourselves
- Paul is teaching them that they reap and sow at the same time
- Paul also communicates that one purpose of God providing for us is so that we might use what we have to give to others
- The overflow of God's provision to us should be used to give to others
- When we trust that God is going to faithfully supply our needs, we do not have to let fear hinder us from giving to others
- Giving is a matter of trust

9:9

- Here is a quote from Psalm 112:9
- The Psalm is teaching that a godly person is willing to "scatter" or give wherever it is needed
- In Greco-Roman world there idea of giving to the poor was looked down upon because they did not foresee any way for them to be re-paid
- The Biblical idea of giving is that you do not need repayment
- The statement "His righteousness endures forever" is teaching that they can trust that God will supply their needs because He is righteous and always will be righteous

- This gives us Paul's interpretation of the Psalm quoted in the previous verse
- The emphasis here is on the fact that God will provide for the generous
- He makes this point by continuing with the metaphor of farming
- What God does in nature, He does for us as well
- Just as God provides the seeds a farmer with seeds to plant which will eventually result in a harvest, so God provides the means for us to sow seeds of generosity
- This language is common throughout the Scriptures
- In fact, this sounds like the language used in the Old Testament
    - **Isaiah 55:10** - "For as the rain and the snow come down from heaven,
      And do not return there without watering the earth
      And making it bear and sprout, And furnishing seed to the sower and bread to the eater
- The seed that God supplies to the sower speaks of wealth that God provides to His people to give to others
- The sowing of the seed speaks of giving
- If God did not provide seed, there could be no sowing of seed
- A person is not able to be generous because he created his own resources, he is able to be generous because God provided
- When Paul says "He who supplies" the word "supplies" is a present active participle which indicates an action that is ongoing (i.e. He is supplying)
- The phrase "bread for food" reminds the Corinthians that God will ensure that their basic needs are met
- A person does not have to cease being generous because of a fear of not having what they need
    - **Psalm 37:25** - I have been young and now I am old,
      Yet I have not seen the righteous forsaken
      Or his ᶦdescendants begging bread.
- The phrase "increase your harvest of righteousness is a phrase take from the book of Hosea
    - **Hosea 10:12** - Sow with a view to righteousness,

> Reap in accordance with kindness;
> Break up your fallow ground, For it is time to seek
> the Lord Until He comes to rain righteousness on
> you.

- The seed that is sown is money that is given. The harvest of righteousness speaks of the result of the generosity
- When Paul speaks of righteousness here he does not necessarily speak of moral rightness, but speaks of taking care of the disadvantaged with what we have been given

9:11

- Once again, Paul makes clear that God enriches for the purpose of liberality
- God blesses people financially, not so they can prosper, but so that they may be able to share it with others
- The error of the rich fool was not sharing his blessings
    - **Luke 12:19** - [19] And I will say to my soul, "Soul, you have many goods laid up for many years *to come*; take your ease, eat, drink *and* be merry.'"
- Paul also makes clear that their generosity results in thanksgiving be given by the recipients of their generosity
- Notice that it is not primarily that thanksgiving flowed to the giver…thanksgiving went to God
- The thanksgiving appropriately went to God because He is ultimately the one that provided the sower with the seed
- The thought of God receiving thanks from others should motivate greater generosity

9:12

- This further explains how the offering was producing thanksgiving
- Paul uses two similar words here
- First, he uses the word translated "ministry"
- Secondly, the word service is the word *leitourgia* (λειτουργία) which can speak of a charitable gift or even the service of a

priest

- He says that their contribution is "fully supplying" the needs of the saints
- The word "fully supplying" means fill up by adding to
- The idea is that they are a part of meeting a real and urgent need
- However, it was not just meeting a physical need, the end result was something spiritually beneficial
- This is the tenth and final time the word "overflowing" is used in 2 Corinthians
- The Corinthian contribution to the Judean church would overflow in thanks being given to God

9:13

- The proof given by this ministry speak of proving the fact that they were really ready to give
- The giving was also a proof of the genuineness of their love
- As Christians, they certainly talked about loving one another, but this type of generosity would have proved that this love was genuine
- It would have spoken volumes that these Gentile Christians were willing to give to these Jewish Christians
- It would have made clear that their love transcended all barriers.
- Love transcends racial barriers, ethnic barriers, language barriers, geographical barriers and cultural barriers
- Verses 11-12 speak about thanksgiving being given to God as a result of this gift
- Verse 13 speaks about two specific ways that the recipients of the gift would glorify God as it relates to the giver of the gift
- First, they would glorify God that the Corinthians were obedient to their confession of the Gospel of Christ
- Paul suggests that their generosity is tied directly to them living out the confession of the Gospel
- The confession speaks of a declaration of Jesus' Lordship and kingship
- The confession that they would have made was about Jesus being the Savior of the world which they were showing they

believed through their giving
- The reason this connection is made to their generosity is because the Corinthian's gift would have shown that they were living out the confession that Jesus is God's Messiah for the whole world and that Jesus breaks down all barriers
- This shows that confession is not just something that you say or repeat, but it is something to be lived out
- Paul is saying that this would erase any doubts the Jewish Christians may have about the sincerity of the faith of the Gentiles
- Second, they would glorify God for the liberality of their contribution
- They would glorify God that these Christians were willing to be so generous

9:14

- The Judean Christian are not just glorifying God for the Corinthian gift, but they are doing two things towards those who would share with them
- First, he says that the Judean Christians are praying for them as well
- While the Judean Christians were in need of financial help, they were giving something that they could give…their prayers on behalf of the saints
- Prayers offered on their behalf is not just a token thing, it is a grand thing
- It is an incredible encouragement when we know others are praying for us
- There is a great lesson here about praying for and supporting God's people all around the world
- Second, he says that they "yearn" for them
- That is that they long to meet them or be with them in Christian fellowship
- Given the tension that previously existed between Jews and Gentiles even in the early days of the church, this is quite profound

- With the statement "because of the surpassing grace of God in you" Paul is pointing out that this generous gift would go a long way to change the outlook of the Jewish Christians towards Gentile Christians

9:15

- Following this incredibly serious appeal for generosity, Paul breaks into a moment of praise
- His doxology is a reminder of God's incredible gift and generosity towards us
- The gift that Paul is speaking of is our salvation that comes through the sacrifice of Jesus on the cross
- Paul calls God's gift on our behalf as "indescribable" gift
- This is the only known usage of the word translated "indescribable" not just in the New Testament, but in Greek literature
- Paul's intent is to focus on the incredible nature of the gift that God has provided
- While the Gentile world taking up a collection to provide for physical needs for others should result in thanksgiving and glorifying God, how much greater the overflow of thanks for such a spiritual blessing
- We are reminded that Christian giving is done with God's gift to us in view
- Our generosity to others is modelled after God's generosity to us
- We get some sense of the result of this plea for a contribution at the end of the book of Romans
    - **Romans 15:26-27** - [26] For Macedonia and Achaia have been pleased to make a contribution for the poor among the saints in Jerusalem. [27] Yes, they were pleased *to do so*, and they are indebted to them. For if the Gentiles have shared in their spiritual things, they are indebted to minister to them also in material things.

2 Corinthians 10

- In the first 9 chapters, we see Paul writing with a very calm tone with the sense that things were trending in the right direction in Corinth
- In chapter 10, there is a change in tone
- The tone becomes much more defensive and strong
- He will spend time correcting them for various errors as well as defending himself from his opponents
- It is for this reason that some have assumed that this is a part of a different letter from Paul which for some reason has been appended to 2 Corinthians
- We do not find any reason to believe that this is some other letter, but rather we believe that it is a part of Paul's original text

10:1

- The issue that he will speak of here is the question of his apparent lack of boldness when he is with the Corinthians face to face
- Paul is rejecting the idea that he is only bold when he writes, but not able to do so when face to face
- As he goes on he will further clarify that if he needs to, he is more than prepared to be bold when he comes and visits them
- Notice that when Paul says, "I who am meek when face to face" that this is not Paul's estimation of things, this is him citing the Corinthian complaint about himself
- The word the NASB translates as "meek" in this statement is not the same as the word Paul uses in this verse to speak of the meekness of Christ
- The word used is the word "humble"
- The Corinthians were accusing him of being lowly or humble when he was with them face to face
- The Corinthians accusation suggests two mistakes
- First, they misstated the reality of the situation
- Second, the misunderstood the place of humility
- While meekness and gentleness may have been perceived as

virtues in Greek culture, humility was not seen as a virtue at all
- What they were putting forth as an attack on Paul's character and portrayed as weakness was actually a virtue on display
- The Corinthians also accused him of being very bold in his writing
- While we do not know the tone of Paul's visits to Corinth, we do know that some of his writing in 1 Corinthians and 2 Corinthians was quite bold
- We can also assume that the missing "harsh" letter would have been very bold
- We also know that Paul threatened at time to come to them in boldness
    - **1 Corinthians 4:19-21** - [19] But I will come to you soon, if the Lord wills, and I shall find out, not the words of those who are arrogant but their power. [20] For the kingdom of God does not consist in words but in power. [21] What do you desire? Shall I come to you with a rod, or with love and a spirit of gentleness?
- The Corinthians accusation is one of cowardliness or some level of duplicity
- However, the attack was not merely a personal one. It was an attempt to undermine his apostleship
- As he introduces the issue, he wants the Corinthians to know that his ministry style is modeled after Jesus' ministry style
- In verses 3-5, he will speak about the weapons of warfare that he uses
- Here, he cites that while he has certain weapons he will use that they are always used with meekness and gentleness
- Meekness and gentleness are very similar traits
- Paul wanted the reader to reminded of how Jesus employed both meekness and gentleness in his ministry
- Jesus constantly displayed meekness
    - **Matthew 11:29** - [29] Take My yoke upon you and learn from Me, for I am gentle (*meek*) and humble in heart, and you will find rest for your souls.

- o **Matthew 21:5** - "Say to the daughter of Zion, 'Behold your King is coming to you, Gentle (*meek*), and mounted on a donkey, Even on a colt, the foal of a beast of burden.'"
- Meekness is a word that had been used to refer to a powerful ruler who was also gentle and benevolent
- Meekness is not weakness or cowardice
- Meekness can be defined as "strength under control"
- Gentleness and meekness together do not suggest some type of passivity
- It was not un-Christlike to be humble, gentle and meek
- It also was not un-Christlike to be bold or to speak boldly to them
- Boldness and humility do not have to be contrasting virtues

10:2

- The tone of Paul's visit with the Corinthians would depend on how they responded to his writing
- Paul prefers to come to them in humility, in meekness and in gentleness
- He prefers a peaceful visit among the Corinthians
- However, he is also perfectly willing to be bold among them if need be
- He says that he is willing to be "courageous against some"
- He is not afraid to confront, expose or rebuke those in error
- The ones Paul says he is willing to courageously confront are those in the church who have suggested that Paul "walks according to the flesh"
- There is some question as to what Paul means by "walks according to the flesh"
- Sometimes this phrase may be used to refer to someone who is immoral
- It is possible that this was an attack on his motives
- It is more likely that the accusation was that Paul was really no different than anyone else
- The accusation the Corinthians were making was that his

humility among them was evidence that he was not really an apostle
- Although Paul is the same as everyone else in many ways, he is different from everyone else in that he is an apostle
- The implication is that what he says and teaches is not the result of studying under some other teacher, but what he teaches he received directly from Christ

10:3

- When Paul says here, "though we walk in the flesh" he means that even though they are people just like everyone else
- He is limited by the body just as everyone else is
- There is a difference though that Paul notes between the apostles and others
- He says that they fight differently
- He says that they "do not war according to the flesh"
- The word for "wage war" comes from the Greek word *strateuó* (στρατεύομαι) can also mean to fight or to serve as a soldier
- He is telling the Corinthians that he might not look like much, but he is serving as a solider
- Perhaps they could not see this because they were looking for the wrong type of solider fighting the wrong kind of battle with the wrong type of weapons
- Paul did not fit their expectation
- It seems surprising that they are almost disappointed that he was not more bold in person
- He does not rely on the same tactics that most people rely on to fight their battles
- He does not depend upon human resources
- He is not using domination, power plays, cunning or deceit to put down his detractors
- He does not suppose a human enemy
- Paul knows that his fight is not with other people
- This reminds us of what Paul told the Ephesians about where his struggle existed
    - **Ephesians 6:12** - For our struggle is not

> against flesh and blood, but against the rulers,
> against the powers, against the world forces of
> this darkness, against the spiritual forces of
> wickedness in the heavenly places.

- Paul's point here is that no person, not even his detractors, is his actual, ultimate enemy
- What a person believes or teaches may be our enemy
- A person may be used by our enemy
- However, no person is the enemy
- Most people in the world do not recognize this spiritual reality so they make people their enemy and the object of their attacks
- While Paul might be accused of being humble and weak, the reality is that he is at war, engaged in a real battle
- The Corinthians cannot see that he is fighting because they expect something altogether different of a person at war

10:4

- The word for "warfare" here is the word *strateia* (στρατεία) which means "campaign"
- By implication, the idea is that this not just a battle or a skirmish, this is a long campaign

- Paul points out that the weapons of their warfare are not of the flesh
- He is not attempting to use physical weapons because the battle is not a physical battle
- He is not using the weapons that a worldly person might wield to win their arguments
- Paul does not use things like slander, trickery, coercion, or deceit to fight or win
- He does not specify what those exact weapons may be, but we can determine some of what he may have in mind
- The Word of God is a weapon
    - **Ephesians 6:17** - [17] And take the helmet of salvation, and the sword of the Spirit, which is the word of God.

- - Hebrews 4:12 - [12] For the word of God is living and active and sharper than any two-edged sword, and piercing as far as the division of soul and spirit, of both joints and marrow, and able to judge the thoughts and intentions of the heart.
- Prayer is a real weapon
  - - Ephesians 6:18 - [18] With all prayer and petition pray at all times in the Spirit, and with this in view, be on the alert with all perseverance and petition for all the saints
- The Gospel is a weapon
  - - Romans 1:16 - [16] For I am not ashamed of the gospel, for it is the power of God for salvation to everyone who believes, to the Jew first and also to the Greek
- Righteousness and godly living is a weapon
  - - 2 Corinthians 6:7 - [7] in the word of truth, in the power of God; by the weapons of righteousness for the right hand and the left
- The weapons that Paul uses are more powerful because they center around God's power, not man's power
- Paul's focus in these verses is not on the nature of the weapons that he uses, but the effect of those weapons
- First, he says that these weapons destroy fortresses
- A fortress is something that is intended to protect from a siege
- Of course, Paul is not speaking of a physical fortress
- He has in mind the idea that his opponents are in midst of the church at Corinth, thinking that they are safe behind the walls of their false arguments
- The fortress being destroyed speaks of the fact that Paul intends to destroy the reason and logic of the arguments used by his opponents
- Perhaps Paul has in mind the wisdom conveyed in Proverbs
  - - Proverbs 21:22 - A wise man scales the city of the might And brings down the stronghold in which they trust.
- It stands out that Paul is not merely on the defensive, he is

picturing himself as being on the offensive
- He is picture himself as laying siege to the safety net that those whom have attacked him stand

10:5

- In verse 5, Paul describes the exact nature of the destruction of the fortresses
- The military campaign is a battle of thoughts taking place on the battlefield of the mind
- We still face battles for the minds of people on a regular basis
- This highlights the fact that what a person believes and teaches matters
- The ideas a person clings to matter
- The truth is worth fighting for
- He will speak of three specific tactics that are used to destroy the fortresses of false ideas and arguments
- First, he says that they are destroying speculations
- So many false teachings and ideas that are spread are built upon faulty speculations
- The phrase "I think" or "I feel" is not a compelling reason to believe something is true. Instead we should form our beliefs based on "God's Word says".
- The word translated "speculations" means "arguments"
- These are the arguments that are used against Paul or against the truth
- This speaks of false philosophies, worldviews and ideologies
- False arguments lead to false conclusions.
- False conclusions lead to false practices
- False arguments get destroyed by true arguments
- True arguments lead to true conclusions
- True conclusions lead to true practices
- True arguments withstand the test of false arguments
- The way that false arguments are destroyed is by silencing those who espouse them or by reasoning against them
- Paul made it a habit to reason with people wherever he travelled
    - **Acts 17:17 -** So he was reasoning in the synagogue

> with the Jews and the God-fearing *Gentiles*, and in the market place every day with those who happened to be present.

- Second, he says that they are destroying every lofty thing raised up against the knowledge of God
- The idea of "every lofty thing" continues the imagery of a siege against a fortress
- The "lofty thing" speaks of a tower or a military high ground
- Paul says that these false ideas are like the high walls of a fortress
- The lofty things are set up against the knowledge of God
- The lofty thing intends to keep the knowledge of God out
- They are ideas that are used to keep the true knowledge of God out because a knowledge of God destroys the ideas hidden further behind the wall
- Third, he says that they are taking thoughts captive
- With the walls destroyed, that makes it possible to take captives
- Paul says that "they take every thought captive"
- This is not about a personal battle within, this depicts a battle against (and for) other people
- It is not people that being taken captive, it is thoughts that are being taken captive
- The picture here is of Paul leading a siege where false thoughts are taken captive
- The purpose of taking thoughts captive is to make those thoughts, which were at one time citizens of false ideas, obedient and loyal to Jesus
- Once again, it is clear that false ideas cannot and do not lead to obedience to Christ

10:6

- Good soldiers are prepared for action
- Paul makes clear that he is ready
- In fact, the picture is like that of a military tribunal or a court martial, ready to punish the disobedient
- Paul does suggest that he wants and needs the church's backing

for this punishment of the disobedient
- Paul is not acting as a slighted preacher who wants to squash an enemy
- He is wanting to deal with the problem of disobedience to the Gospel

10:7

- When Paul says that they are looking at things "as they are outwardly" he is accusing them of seeing things in a worldly way
- When one looks at things outwardly they may regard the wisdom of God as foolishness (1 Corinthians 1:18)
- Perhaps it was that they were just looking at the outward appearance
- Perhaps they were using worldly criteria to measure Paul
- Paul also calls for some serious examination of their standing
- He calls on those who claim to belong to Christ to test whether this is true
- He is placing a challenge upon his own opponents
- His opponents in Corinth certainly claimed to belong to Christ
- Here, when he speaks of "belonging to Christ" he does not mean belonging to Christ as a Christian
- The problem that the Corinthian opponents of Paul had was not that Paul was not a Christian, it was calling into question his authority and apostleship
- These people claimed to belong to Christ in a more special way than simply as a Christian
- They were confident in themselves and in their special standing with Christ
- They also would infer that means that Paul did not belong to Christ in any special way
- They would reject that he had authority over them
- Perhaps their argument was that "Paul did not look special or impressive" when they saw him face to face
- Perhaps they expected an apostle to be more impressive in demeanor or in his use of authority

- Paul lets them know that they should also understand that Paul and the apostles belong to Christ in a unique and special way
- And as an apostle, he belongs to Christ as a servant and an ambassador

10:8

- Paul now speaks about his own authority
- In fact, here we have Paul boasting about his authority
- The idea of Paul boasting is a prominent concept in the remainder of this letter
- This is not Paul arrogantly bragging
- This is a case of Paul being backed into a corner and having to list his credentials
- Paul certainly had authority as an apostle
- There were some who did not accept that authority or submit to that authority
- Those is positions of leadership have an element of authority that should be respected
- Notice that Paul said where his authority comes from
- His authority did not come from the people because he did not receive his position through an election of a vote
- His authority did not come from himself because he did not seize power
- His authority came from the Lord because the Lord set him apart as an apostle
- He adds that the Lord gave Him that authority not for destroying them
- Although Paul may have to come an punish disobedience, the purpose of that is still constructive not destructive
- Authority should never be used for tearing down
- Sometimes authority requires discipline, but even that discipline is for building up
- This also appears to contrast Paul's use of authority versus that of his opponents
- His opponents used authority to divide and tear down
- If what Paul is saying is true, the Corinthian opponents have no

basis to attack Paul

10:9

- The purpose of Paul's letters was not to incite fear among his readers
- He was not striving to terrify them into obedience
- Paul means that he is not abusing his power
- Also, he means that he is not writing threats that are empty

10:10

- Here, Paul reveals more specific details of what those opponents of his in the church were saying about him
- We do not know exactly how Paul learned of the exact nature of the criticism
- They were calling into question two basic things about Paul: his physical presence and his oratorical ability
- First, they attacked his physical presence
- They called his presence "unimpressive"
- The word used for "unimpressive" means "weak" or "sickly"
- It is possible that by speaking of his "physical presence" that the Corinthian opponents were complaining about the way that he appeared
- It is fair to assume that by this point in time, Paul's suffering, persecution and work had taken a toll on his body
- In a second century writing called *Acts of Paul and Thecla*, Paul is described as "a man small of stature, with a bald head and crooked legs, in a good state of body, with eyebrows meeting and nose somewhat hooked, full of friendliness."
- But it is also quite possible that this is not just about the way that Paul looked
- The issue with his physical presence also speaks of the way that Paul carried himself
- He had already pointed to the fact that he came to the humbly
- Perhaps it was this humility in the way that he carried himself that would have been such an issue for them

- Remember, Corinth was a deeply Hellenistic (Greek) culture which viewed things quite differently than Hebrew cultures
- People of authority were expected to be more commanding in their presence
- Second, they criticized his speech
- They called his speech "contemptible"
- The word "contemptible" is the Greek word *exoutheneó* (ἐξουθενέω) means "to be counted as nothing"
- The ancient world placed a high value on oratory ability
- Perhaps some in the church would have expected an apostle to be more smooth in his speaking ability
- The question was not about his ability to carry a logical point or argument
- In fact, the issue for Paul's detractors seems to be that they senses a disconnect between the way that he wrote and the way that he appeared
- They would describe his letters to them as being "weighty and strong"
- It is likely that they assumed that his oratory ability would make him come across uneducated
- Furthermore, the attack may be that if he were really an apostle he would be more dynamic than he is in person
- The attack is once again on his authority and his apostleship
- They would expect someone with that kind of authority to act differently than he did

10:11

- Paul speaks directly to his critics in this verse
- As Paul gives a defense of himself, notice that he is not defending against the substance of the attacks, he defends against the implications of them
- He does not try to explain himself to his critics either
- He simply defends himself against a charge of hypocrisy of any kind
- There is no difference between who Paul is when he writes versus when he is present among them

- His goal in writing and in his presence among them was always the same
- It is one thing for some to question his style, it is an altogether different thing to question his character
- In 1 Corinthians, Paul dealt with factions who preferred one preacher of another
- Here, he is quite bold because he is defending his character and his authority as an apostle

10:12

- Paul will use a little bit of sarcasm in his own defense
- He says, "we are not so bold to compare ourselves…"
- The word that the NASB translates "bold" comes from the Greek word *talmao* (τολμάω) which means to dare. It carries the idea of pushing oneself forward or "putting it all on the line"
- So, here, he is saying that he will dare to compare himself with those who commend themselves in defense of his apostleship
- The sarcasm is that while this type of comparison game is not Paul's method, he does make comparison here in a sarcastic way
- The difference between Paul and his critics is that they employ self-commendation to tear down their rivals
- This word for comparison (*sugkrino*), was often used as a rhetorical exercise as a method of comparing oneself with other teachers as a way of attracting students
- People in that day assumed that there was a limited amount of honor to go around so they competed viciously for a piece of the honor
- As a result, character attacks were a very common way to shame someone else
- His critics were constantly comparing themselves to others
- In doing so, they were forced to put others down to build themselves up
- Paul was the target of their attacks
- These critics set themselves up as the standard by which they should be compared
- They were using the wrong criteria to judge Paul

- Of course, they thought that their abuse of their authority was the standard by which everyone else should be judged

10:13

- Paul clarifies that he is not going to get sucked into a comparison game that tears others down
- Now, Paul has spent time boasting about his credentials as an apostle
- Here, he is not saying that he will not compare at all or that he will not boast at all
- He says, "we will not boast beyond our measure"
- The phrase "beyond our measure" means beyond that which is measured
- Paul is not trying to use worldly criteria to make a comparison with others
- Paul is willing to measure himself with a measurable standard
- The NASB speaks of the "sphere" that God has given him
- The word "sphere" is the Greek word *kanon* (κανών) which was a measuring rod. It means "the standard", the ruler, or it can even speak of a province or area
- This word came to be used to describe the books that were included in the Bible
- The standard that he points to is his success on the mission field that God placed him in
- Paul is speaking here of his sphere of influence
- The measure that Paul suggests should be used to compare or to prove oneself is faithfulness to the task that God has given that person
- Paul can only be faithful in what has been assigned to him
- The claim Paul is making is not only that he has been faithful in the places God has commissioned him, but also that Corinth was a place that God commissioned him to go to

10:14

- This explains a little more of what Paul meant when he spoke of

the sphere that God apportioned to him
- It also explains more of the criticism against Paul
- It would seem that some in the church suggested that Corinth was not Paul's territory
- The thing the Corinthian critics are saying is that he does not have authority in Corinth because it lies outside his jurisdiction
- Paul is saying that he did not go beyond what God commissioned him to go when he went to Corinth
- Paul reminds the church that he was the first to come to them with the Gospel
- In other words, Paul is the one who established the church
- He is not some Johnny-come-lately to Corinth
- These critics are the intruders, not Paul
- Paul is implying that these false apostles in Corinth are usurpers of authority
- They were coming into this church and stealing the church
- This is often what false teachers do. They are more likely to steal than to start
- Jesus said this would be case
  - **John 10:1** - "Truly, truly, I say to you, he who does not enter by the door into the fold of the sheep, but climbs up some other way, he is a thief and a robber.

10:15

- Paul makes a similar point to the one he made in verse 13 about not boasting beyond limits
- He says that he is not boasting of other men's labor
- He is not claiming that the successes of someone else's were his own and evidence of something special he had done
- The message is that the Corinthian opponents were boasting of someone else's labor
- They were taking credit for Paul's labor in Corinth and then using it as a means to boast of themselves while putting Paul down
- When he speaks of the hope of their faith growing, he means two things

- First, he means that they settle these issues in the church so that he can direct his focus elsewhere
- Paul is having to spend a lot of time dealing with the church at Corinth which is causing him to not reach more new people with the Gospel
- Secondly, his hope is that as their faith grows and they send missionaries out that his sphere will increase with these spiritual grandchildren
- The word "enlarged" means to "grow greatly"
- Paul is hoping for an enlarged sphere of influence
- Like a good mission minded person, Paul's hope is to expand his effectiveness to more and more people

10:16

- Paul's goal is for his influence to spready far beyond Corinth
- His desire for this is not to exert more authority or to have more power
- Paul's desire is to reach more and more people with the Gospel
- In Romans, Paul spoke of his desire to go to both Spain and Rome with the Gospel
  - **Romans 15:23-29** - [23] but now, with no further place for me in these regions, and since I have had for many years a longing to come to you [24] whenever I go to Spain—for I hope to see you in passing, and to be helped on my way there by you, when I have first enjoyed your company for a while— [25] but now, I am going to Jerusalem serving the saints. [26] For Macedonia and Achaia have been pleased to make a contribution for the poor among the saints in Jerusalem. [27] Yes, they were pleased *to do so,* and they are indebted to them. For if the Gentiles have shared in their spiritual things, they are indebted to minister to them also in material things. [28] Therefore, when I have finished this, and have put my seal on this fruit of theirs, I will go on by way of you to Spain. [29] I know that when I

> come to you, I will come in the fullness of the blessing of Christ.

- Once again, Paul accuses the Corinthian critics of boasting in someone else's labor

10:17

- Paul now uses Scripture to rebuke those in Corinth who were boasting in themselves in order to tear Paul down
- The quotation comes from Jeremiah 9:24
    - **Jeremiah 9:23-24** - [23] Thus says the Lord, "Let not a wise man boast of his wisdom, and let not the mighty man boast of his might, let not a rich man boast of his riches; [24] but let him who boasts boast of this, that he understands and knows Me, that I am the Lord who exercises lovingkindness, justice and righteousness on earth; for I delight in these things," declares the Lord.
- Paul's point is that these people have not been giving credit to the Lord
- Paul's boasting was always in what the Lord has done through him

10:18

- Paul follows this up by pointing out the fallacy of commending oneself
- He saying that the one commending themselves is not approved
- That is they are not approved by God
- It is only God's approval that matters
- The word used for "approval" is a word that was used for the testing of metals
- The person who is doing God's word should give God the credit
- The Lord commends the person who boasts in the Lord and gives God the credit

2 Corinthians 11

11:1

- Paul has been forced to defend himself to the congregation and to his critics
- Paul tells the church to "bear with him" as he spends some time boasting
- Paul was never a fan of self-commendation
- In fact, here, he will say that this type of commendation is foolishness
- One of the differences between Paul and his critics is that he admits that self-commendation is foolishness, they do not
- The word "fool" and "foolish" are key concepts in this chapter

11:2

- Paul speaks of the issues here with the metaphor of a betrothal
- In the metaphor, Paul is pictured as the father of the church who has arranged this marriage
- He as the father, has betrothed the church to a husband
- The husband here is Christ
- The church at Corinth was betrothed to one husband, not many husbands
- The Jewish understanding of a betrothal was that it was the first stage of marriage
- A betrothal was a legally binding agreement
- This type of engagement was not something that could be broken easily
- It was only through getting a bill of divorce that a betrothal could be ended
- It was considered adultery for a betrothed person to have any type of sexual relations with another person
- The picture here is of the church in Corinth being the bride in waiting for her husband Christ
- The responsibility of the betrothed bride was to stay pure
- In the Jewish culture, the father had a responsibility to preserve

his daughter's purity (Deuteronomy 22:13-21)
- Paul sees it as his responsibility to preserve this purity until the marriage takes place at Christ's coming
- Paul picks up on this idea and says "he is jealous with a godly jealousy"
- Paul feels that their moral purity is at risk by their relationship to the Judaizers in the church

11:3

- Speaking to the church, Paul lets them know that he is afraid that they might be deceived
- He cites the example of how the serpent deceived Eve
- Eve was deceived by craftiness and lies of the serpent
- The ones potentially deceiving the church are Paul's critics or Judaizers
- The battle is in the mind
- The serpent tricked Eve in her mind with the lust of the eye, the lust of the flesh and the boastful pride of life
- These teachers in Corinth was attempting to lead their minds astray
- If their minds are lead astray, their heart and actions will follow
- The thing that they were in danger of being led away from was their devotion to Christ
- Paul first refers to the simplicity of their devotion
- Second, he refers to the purity of their devotion to Christ
- The idea that Paul is communicating is that these critics in the church were not just attacking Paul, but they were causing some in Corinth to have a less devoted form of faith in Christ

11:4

- Paul points out some of the errors of his critics in Corinth
- He will mention three possible errors that the Corinthian church should be on the guard against
- Notice also that these opponents of Paul come to the church at Corinth whereas Paul is sent

- These are quick ways to identify a false teacher
- First, they preach a different Jesus
- We are not certain in what way they preached another Jesus
- They preached a Jesus that was different from the one they were betrothed to
- They preached a Jesus with a different character
- Perhaps some of the preaching in Paul's mind disregarded the weakness of Jesus in His death
  - **2 Corinthians 13:4** - [4] For indeed He was crucified because of weakness, yet He lives because of the power of God. For we also are weak in Him, yet we will live with Him because of the power of God *directed* toward you.
- Perhaps the teachers even failed to emphasize His death
- Paul preached Jesus crucified, risen and reigning as Lord
- Second, they preach a different spirit
- I do not believe here the focus is on the Holy Spirit
- I believe that he is speaking of someone coming and preaching with a different spirit or attitude
- The Judaizers preaching led to a spirit of fear rather than freedom
- Third, they preach a different Gospel
- In Galatians 1, Paul warns about those who preach another Gospel
  - **Galatians 1:8** - [8] But even if we, or an angel from heaven, should preach to you a gospel contrary to what we have preached to you, he is to be accursed!
- They added conditions to the Gospel
- Perhaps they added to or even took away from the message of the Gospel
- A substitute Gospel is no gospel at all
- It is hard to imagine anyone resembling a Christian differing on those three subjects
- There is an inherent danger is new teaching that we should always be on guard against
- He says that the church at Corinth "bears" this
- They apparently were putting up with these people in the church

- Paul is suggesting that the church of Corinth should be with him in a greater way than they bear with these false teachers

11:5

- It is likely that some would have regarded Paul as a lesser apostle than the others
- Paul suggests here that he is in no way inferior to them
- It seems odd when he says this because elsewhere he humbly says he is the "lead of the apostles"
  - **1 Corinthians 15:9-10** - [9] For I am the least of the apostles, and not fit to be called an apostle, because I persecuted the church of God. [10] But by the grace of God I am what I am, and His grace toward me did not prove vain; but I labored even more than all of them, yet not I, but the grace of God with me.
- Here, Paul is not speaking of the apostles of Jesus
- In this verse he refers to them as "most eminent apostles"
- The word for "eminent" is the Greek word *hyperlian* (Ὑπερλίαν) which means superlative
- He is speaking of a group that he labels "super apostles"
- This is a term probably coined by Paul to refer to these opponents in the church
- These people were suggesting that Paul did not have authority, that he was not an apostle and that they were better than Paul
- While Paul was a humble man, he was not going to idly sit by and let these people usurp his authority and lead the church astray

11:6

- The comparison Paul is drawing between himself and these people he had dubbed "superapostles"
- He will once again go back to the attacks that they have made upon him
- First, he will focus on the attack against his oratorical ability
- One of the main attacks against Paul was about his speech

- The Greek culture would have placed a high value on oratory ability
- Paul acknowledges that he is not the most dynamic orator
- The issue though is a style issue, not a content issue
- I would argue that Paul is being somewhat modest in this concession
- The problem was not with Paul it was with the Corinthians
- Perhaps he did not stylistically measure up with Greek orators or even these superapostles
- Perhaps they mistook his humility for weakness
- While he admits to not being the best communicator, he claims that he does not lack in knowledge
- Certainly he had knowledge of the Scripture that he had gained throughout his life
- Perhaps he was even a naturally gifted student
- However, this speaks of knowledge that God has given to him specifically as an apostle
- Paul had special revealed knowledge of the Gospel

11:7

- The second attack Paul references is the criticism of his practice of not taking pay from the church
- Paul made reference of this choice in 1 Corinthians (1 Corinthians 9:4-18)
- Paul not only did not take a salary from the church, but he worked as a tentmaker to supplement his income
- Paul uses some exaggeration to making his point
- His asks the rhetorical question of whether he was sinning by doing this?
- The obvious answer would be "no"
- Paul makes evident that the issue that they had was his humility
- Paul says that he humbled himself so that the Corinthians may be exalted
- God says, "he who humbles himself will be exalted"
- Paul wanted to offer the Gospel free of charge so that no one could falsely accuse him

* Paul did not actually steal from any churches
* He means this sarcastically
* He took money from the churches in order to support his work in Corinth and in other places
* That money certainly could have been used for other things
* We know that he drew some support from Philippi
    * **Philippians 4:15-16** - [15] You yourselves also know, Philippians, that at the [i]first preaching of the gospel, after I left Macedonia, no church shared with me in the matter of giving and receiving but you alone; [16] for even in Thessalonica you sent *a gift* more than once for my needs
* If he was drawing support from churches in Macedonia, we remember that those particular congregations were very poor compared to Corinth
* Paul also noted in 1 Corinthians that he had every right to expect pay for his Gospel work
* Other supporting churches willingly gave to Paul to support his Gospel work
* Evidently, Paul's practice was to work a job and support himself rather than take money from the church he was preaching, but he was willing to draw support from other churches for this work
* The word "robbed" here comes from the Greek word *sulao* (συλάω)
* The word was used to refer to the practice of a soldier on the battlefield plundering items from dead soldiers
* The word for "support" is a word that was used to speak of a soldier's pay

* Paul is vouching for his own character and integrity here
* He lets them know that when he was in financial need during his time in Corinth, the way that need was met was from other churches

- As their preacher was in need, they allowed other churches to meet that need
- Paul is not necessarily faulting the church for that; he says that he never wanted to be a burden
- The word for "burden" is the Greek word *katanarkao* (καταναρκάω) which was a medical term meaning "to make numb" or "to paralyze"
- The second time the word "burden" appears in this verse it is a different word (*abares*) which will mean "not a weight"
- One has to wonder why Paul felt that receiving support from the church he preached at would have been a burden rather than a blessing
- The only time Paul asked the Corinthians for money was when the money was for other people
- Apparently, some of Paul's greatest support came from the poverty stricken churches in Macedonia

10:10

- The phrase "as surely as Christ's truth is in me" is the wording of an oath
- Paul speaks of the truth of Christ being in him as a vessel
- Here, Paul is once again speaking of the fact that Christ's truth is in him in a special way as an apostle
- The boast that Paul speaks of here is the boasting of his working without accepting pay
- He is saying that he is not going to stop this practice of not asking for pay
- Remember, Corinth is the capital of Achaia

10:11

- The "why" speaks of the boasting being stopped
- It is not just speaking of the continuing to boast, but the continuation of his practice to not ask for pay
- Perhaps his detractors were saying that Paul's not taking pay was because he did not love them

- We even understand that refusing to accept a gift can be seen as offensive
- Paul says that his motivation is because he does love them
- He adds that God can testify to the fact that he loves the church

11:12

- Paul states that another reason that he refused to accept payment from the church is to "cut off opportunity" from his opponents
- The word "opportunity" speaks of a launching point
- It refers to one of the criticisms that the critics were using to elevate themselves
- The word also was used to speak of a base of operations
- Paul is hitting at the foundation of the difference between himself and these superapostles
- The issue speaks to their motives
- Paul was not in it for himself. These critics were self-serving
- Paul was using this whole line of boasting to eliminate their arguments against him (and for themselves)
- Specifically, Paul is suggesting that his practice of not accepting payment was in part to contrast himself with them
- The argument was to prove that the opponents in Corinth were not his equals
- They had worked hard through boasting to set themselves up as superior to Paul or at the very least as being apostles themselves
- Preaching for the church at Corinth without pay was a way to undercut their boast
- Certainly, these people would not have preached the Gospel free of charge
- Paul is putting for sacrificial service as a mark of apostleship

11:13

- Paul now takes the gloves off and describes his critics very plainly
- He will use three phrases to describe these opponents
- First, he says that they are false apostles (*pseudoapostolos*)

- Earlier, he had sarcastically spoken of them as "super apostles"
- As far as we know, they did not even meet the qualifications for an apostle found in Acts 1
    - **Acts 1:21-21 -** [21] Therefore it is necessary that of the men who have accompanied us all the time that the Lord Jesus went in and out among us
      — [22] beginning with the baptism of John until the day that He was taken up from us—one of these *must* become a witness with us of His resurrection."
- Paul calls some people "false brothers" as well
    - **2 Corinthians 11:26 -** [26] I have been on frequent journeys, in dangers from rivers, dangers from robbers, dangers from my countrymen, dangers from the Gentiles, dangers in the city, dangers in the wilderness, dangers on the sea, dangers among false brethren
    - **Galatians 2:4 -** [4] But it was because of the false brethren secretly brought in, who had sneaked in to spy out our liberty which we have in Christ Jesus, in order to bring us into bondage.
- Just because a person claims a title does not mean that is what they really are
- Jesus warned about false prophets
    - **Matthew 7:15 -** [15] "Beware of the false prophets, who come to you in sheep's clothing, but inwardly are ravenous wolves.
- Jesus also warned about false Christs
    - **Matthew 24:24 -** [24] For false Christs and false prophets will arise and will show great signs and wonders, so as to mislead, if possible, even the elect.
- Now, he says that they are false apostles
- Second, he says that they are deceitful workers
- Notice that they are workers (*ergatai*), but their agenda is deceit
- The word "workers" is often used to speak of missionaries or leaders in the church
    - **Matthew 10:10 -** [10] or a bag for *your* journey, or

> even two coats, or sandals, or a staff; for the worker
> is worthy of his support.
>   o **1 Timothy 5:18** - [18] For the Scripture says, "You
>   shall not muzzle the ox while he is threshing," and
>   "The laborer is worthy of his wages."

- There is a definite issue with the motives of these opponents
- Third, he says that they disguise themselves as apostles of Christ
- These opponents evidently claim to be apostles of Christ
- These "false apostles" would have gone to great lengths to present themselves as true apostles
- The word "disguise" is the Greek word *metaschématizó* (μετασχηματίζω) which means to change the outward appearance
- Here, the idea is that these false apostles are covering up their real motives and agenda
- With these statements, it is not possible for the reader to remain neutral about these people
- It also would obliterate any logic that may have compelled them to bear with these people or that they could co-exist in the church
- Either Paul's description is true or it is not
- The reader could not believe what Paul says is true and continue to tolerate these people at the same time

11:14

- In this verse, Paul speaks further about the desire these people have to hide their true motives
- He suggests that it should not be surprising that these people go to such great lengths to do this
- The reason he gives is because Satan himself disguises himself as an angel of light
- The implication here is that these people are simply doing the tactics of the one who they really serve
- If Satan disguises himself as an angel of light, we might expect his servants to do the same thing
- The Greek (present participle) makes clear that this is not just a

tactic Satan has used, but it is one that Satan continually uses to serve his purposes
- Satan can use a disguise of righteousness to accomplish his purposes
- Jewish tradition spoke of Satan appearing to Eve in the Garden "in the form of a beautiful angel and singing hymns like the angels" (*The Apocalypse of Moses 7:2*)[2]

11:15

- The overall point is that while Satan can certainly work openly with clear evil, he also has minions at work within the church and pretending to be righteous
- Paul is specifically suggesting that his opponents in Corinth are evil people disguised as servants of Christ
- He says they disguise themselves as servants of "righteousness"
- In 3:9, Paul said that the New Covenant was a ministry of righteousness
- These people claim to be servants of righteousness, but in reality they serve Satan
- We do not know if they knew that they were in league with Satan, but Paul says that their goal is the same as Satan's goal
- These people will also share the same end as Satan
- Paul makes it very clear that these opponents in the church are going to be judged for their actions
- This does not mean that every false teacher is a direct minion of Satan as there are some people who are sincere although sincerely wrong
- However, this does make very clear that even withing the sphere of Christianity that there are people who outwardly look the part, but the reality is that they are disguised as servants of God
- Christians should always be on the guard against false teachers

11:16

- Here, Paul goes back to the idea of the foolishness of boasting that he introduced in 11:1

- Although some may see what Paul is doing here as a foolish way to speak, but has a reason for his boasting
- The phrase "receive me" means that he wants them to listen to him even though they may find his line of reasoning that of a fool
- In fact, by saying, "receive me as a fool", he is suggesting that they should give him the same attention they give to the fools that they have been bearing with

11:17-18

- Paul certainly understands that boasting like this is not ideal
- This is why he refers to it as "foolishness"
- Most people who boast do not even realize what they are doing when they boast
- Paul is fully aware that this type of boasting is not the best way to argue
- However, it was necessary to prove a point to his critics and in order to defend himself
- He is using the same style that his opponents may use to elevate themselves
- They often boast "according the flesh"
- That phrase means "the way the world does"
- It speaks of the arrogance that undergirds the boasting of most people
- The Corinthians and Paul's detractors saw Paul's contrasting humility as a negative thing
- And since others boast like that, Paul says, "I can do the same thing"
- We will see that Paul gives visible, tangible evidence in his boasting in the following verses whereas his opponents cannot

11:19

- Remember that "wisdom" is a key concept for the Corinthian culture
- They really prided themselves on wisdom

- So, when Paul speaks of them being "wise" here, he means it somewhat sarcastically
- Paul sometimes uses the terms "wise" and "fool" sarcastically
    - **1 Corinthians 4:10** - ¹⁰ We are fools for Christ's sake, but you are prudent in Christ; we are weak, but you are strong; you are distinguished, but we are without honor.
- He says that "you being wise tolerate fools gladly"
- He obviously has in mind the foolish opponents that they have tolerated
- His point is that maybe he needs to indulge in the same foolish style as his opponents use for the Corinthians to tolerate him
- They did not tolerate Paul when he was wise in his approach, so maybe they would tolerate him more if he acted the fool like the opponents

11:20

- Paul will speak of the irony of their tolerance of these people
- They tolerate these people in spite of the way that they act among them and treat them
- The things mentioned here are descriptions of these Judaizers, but they are also contrasting to how Paul was among them
- They tolerate people who mistreat them and lead them astray
- The picture is of tolerating people that no person should tolerate
- The whole irony is that they are more tolerant of these people than they are of Paul
- He will mention five different things that describe the people the Corinthians have been tolerating
- First, they enslave
- Their legalistic doctrine is enslaving
- They created rules and laws that God never bound upon people
- They expect actions and response that they themselves cannot measure up to
- Paul used this same word in Galatians to describe the Judaizer's attempt to undermine Christian freedom
    - **Galatians 2:4** - ⁴ But *it was* because of the false

> brethren secretly brought in, who had sneaked in to spy out our liberty which we have in Christ Jesus, in order to bring us into bondage.

- Second, they devour
- The word for "devour" is a word that was used of the way one species of animal might prey upon and then devour its prey
- Jesus speaks of people as devouring other people through their teaching
    - **Mark 12:40** - [40] who devour widows' houses, and for appearance's sake offer long prayers; these will receive greater condemnation.
- Third, they take advantage
- The word "take advantage" has in mind catching an animal in a snare
- The idea is that the church is being taken advantage of by sinister people
- Fourth, they exalt themselves
- They forcibly exalt themselves over and lord it over the Corinthians
- This is quite the contrast between them and Paul's humility among them
- He said earlier that he did not take pay and humbled himself so that the church might be exalted
- Paul was a picture of humility and service. These superapostles were a picture of domination
- Fifth, they hit them in the face
- This does not speak of some type of literal abuse, but rather the insulting behavior

11:21

- It would probably be necessary to break this verse into two different parts because it seems that verse 21 contains to ideas
- First, Paul will speaks about his weakness
- The first part of this verse is full of sarcasm
- Paul is suggesting that if the definition of strength is what is seen in his rivals, then he is actually weak

- If it is weak to be humble and not tear others down, then he admits to weakness
- By the worlds standards, Paul and the other apostles are probably actually weak
- It is actually in Paul's weakness that God approves
- Paul is proud to be weak if weak is defined as the Corinthian rivals would define it
- Second, Paul will speak about his boldness in the boasting he is going to do
- Paul is about to really launch into the boasting which he hinted at earlier
- He is willing to engage in some boldness in this boasting
- However, he acknowledges that this whole line of reasoning is less than ideal
- In fact, he says plainly that engaging in bold boasting is foolishness
- In fact, some of the criteria that Paul will list as a means of boasting are not the real measure of his quality or qualifications as an apostle
- Paul is not suggesting that these are legitimate means of comparison
- Despite some reluctance to argue with his rivals on their level, Paul will boast of his sufferings and achievements

11:22

- Paul's list of achievements are filled with some of his hardships
- Oddly enough, most Greeks would have seen Paul's list of achievements are further evidence of his weakness
- The first thing he speaks about is his lineage
- It is interesting that Paul will speak of his lineage and heritage considering this something that one is born into, not something one has any say about
- However, the argument of coming from good stock would have been a typical Jewish and Hellenistic way of arguing
- He will use three different rhetorical questions which ask the same basic question

- The question points straight to his Jewish roots and ethnicity
- His questions are directed at his rivals directly. He says, "are they…?"
- Remember, the rivals in the church at Corinth are some type of Judaizers who emphasize Jewishness and maintaining the Law to go along with Christianity
- They would have placed supreme value in their Jewishness as a proof of their loyalty to Christ and their superiority to others
- In a comparison game, Paul does not lack in having Jewish roots
- First, he asks "are they Hebrews?"
- This probably is emphasizing that Paul is full-blooded Hebrew
- Not only that but he is Hebrew as opposed to Greek
- He had been raised in Palestine, not is Greek culture
- He spoke the Hebrew or Aramaic language
- In Acts 6, there was some dispute and distinction made between Hebrew and Hellenists
    - **Acts 6:1** - Now at this time while the disciples were increasing *in number*, a complaint arose on the part of the Hellenistic *Jews* against the *native* Hebrews, because their widows were being overlooked in the daily serving *of food*.
- Hellenistic speaks of Greek speaks Jews who were now Christians while Hebrew speaks of Aramaic speaking Jews who were now Christians
- He meets the criteria that these Judaizers would have placed value in
- Conversely, Paul is not actually placing spiritual value in his Hebrew origin
- Second, he asks, "are the Israelites?"
- The idea here is that he can go back and connect himself to one of the tribes
- We know that Paul came from the tribe of Benjamin
    - **Philippians 3:5 -** ⁵circumcised the eighth day, of the nation of Israel, of the tribe of Benjamin, a Hebrew of Hebrews; as to the Law, a Pharisee
- Third, Paul says, "are they descendants of Abraham?"
- This means that Paul can trace his genealogy back to Abraham

- Some of the Jews made the same claim to Jesus
    - **John 8:39** - [39] They answered and said to Him, "Abraham is our father." Jesus said to them, "If you are Abraham's children, do the deeds of Abraham.
- Paul, in Galatians, will speaks of Gentiles followers of Jesus being of the seed of Abraham
    - **Galatians 3:7** - [7] Therefore, be sure that it is those who are of faith who are sons of Abraham.
- Paul is not suggesting that one's descent is anything worth using as a means of superiority. He is using their own criteria to prove his superiority to his rivals
- His point is that these rivals cannot make a valid claim of superiority over Paul based on their ethnicity, heritage or descent
- Even if their lineage really counted for something (and it doesn't), Paul can match them

11:23

- He introduces another rhetorical question
- This time the question is "are they servants of Christ?"
- This was obviously a claim that these rivals were making
- Here, Paul does not dispute that they are servants of Christ
- Although we know that they were not TRUE servants of Christ
- He says that he is "more" a servant of Christ than these people are
- The word for "more" here is the word *"huper"* which reminds us of the phrase Paul coined for the rivals; superapostles (*huper apostlon*)
- What he disputes is that they have any ground to claim to be greater servants of Christ than Paul
- In fact, Paul is going to say that if we want to quantify service to Christ with worldly criteria, he wins
- We get the sense of the frustration of Paul as he makes these points
- He even says, "I speak as if insane"
- This word is different that the word he used to describe his line

- of reasoning in verse 21 when he said it is "foolishness" (*aphron*)
- The word for "insane" is the word *paraphroneo* (παραφρονέω) which literally means "beside myself" or it can mean "deranged"
- He also will explain how it is that he can claim to be "more a servant of Christ"
- Of course, this is just taking worldly criteria into account
- First, he says that he has more labors than the superapostles have
- The idea here is that he has worked harder for the cause of Christ
- The word Paul uses for "far more" means that it goes "way past"
- If you just lined up Paul's accomplishments for the Gospel to that of the superapostles, Paul argues that he has worked harder and accomplished more
- Second, he says that he has more imprisonments that the superapostles have
- This speaks of his imprisonments that came as a result of preaching the Gospel
- At the time of this writing, we know only that Paul was in jail for a short time in Philippi (Acts 16:23-40)
- This does not mean that there were not more imprisonments, just that we do not have record of all of them
- Paul would later have a two year Roman imprisonment
- There is an ancient document which is called First Clement, which was composed before the end of the first century which suggests that Paul faced seven different imprisonments[3]
- He has not just labored, but he has suffered for the cause of Christ
- He says that he had beaten more times that he could number
- In addition, he speaks of being often in danger of death

11:24

- Following this he expounds on his sufferings by citing more specifics
- In these verses Paul will catalog some of his sufferings
- In verses 24-25, he will cite four specific ways he suffered along

with the number of times that particular suffering occurred
- First, he says that he on five occasions received 39 lashes at the hands of the Jews
- Jesus warned his disciples that this would happen to them
    - **Matthew 10:17** - [17] But beware of men, for they will hand you over to *the* courts and scourge you in their synagogues
- Forty lashes was the maximum punishment permitted under the Law
    - **Deuteronomy 25:1-3** - "If there is a dispute between men and they go to [a]court, and the judges decide their case, and they justify the righteous and condemn the wicked, [2] then it shall be if the wicked man deserves to be beaten, the judge shall then make him lie down and be beaten in his presence with the number of stripes according to his guilt. [3] He may beat him forty times *but* no more, so that he does not beat him with many more stripes than these and your brother is not degraded in your eyes.
- The number thirty-nine was used to allow for miscounting
- It was expected that 26 of those stripes would be across the individual's back, while 13 went across the chest
- David Garland says, "According to the *Mishnah*, thirty-six sins, including blasphemy, warranted being cut off from the people without warning. But flogging averted both a harsher punishment at the hands of God and being cut off from the people."
- If this is the case, it is possible, even probable that Paul consented to flogging five times simply to maintain an influence and audience among the Jews

11:25

- Second, he says that he on three occasions was beaten with rods
- These would have been beatings in the public square as deemed by the local magistrates
- The offender would have been hit with heavy birchwood rods

- The only record we have in Acts in the beating Paul and Silas
  received in Philippi
    - **Acts 16:22-23** - [22] The crowd rose up together
      against them, and the chief magistrates tore
      their robes off them and proceeded to order *them* to
      be beaten with rods. [23] When they had struck them
      with many blows, they threw them into prison,
      commanding the jailer to guard them securely
- These types of beating were not allowed from Roman citizens
- It is this point that caused an issue in Philippi (Acts 16:35-40)
- Third, he says that on one occasion he underwent stoning
- This event is likely the event that took place in Lystra and is
  recorded in Acts 14
    - **Acts 14:19** - [19] But Jews came from Antioch
      and Iconium, and having won over the crowds,
      they stoned Paul and dragged him out of the city,
      supposing him to be dead.
- Fourth, he says that on three separate occasions he was
  shipwrecked
- The only shipwreck we have recorded in the one we read of in
  Acts 27, which happened after he wrote 2 Corinthians
- It is very clear that these types of suffering would have taken a
  physical toll on Paul
    - **Galatians 6:17** - [17] From now on let no one cause
      trouble for me, for I bear on my body the brand-
      marks (*stigmata*) of Jesus.

11:26

- Paul's frequent journeys speaks of his mission trips and travels
  to spread the Gospel
- Paul would have travelled thousands of miles, mostly on foot
- The key to this is that Paul faced danger at every turn
- He speaks of eight specific dangers that he regularly faced in the
  midst of his journeys
- First, he says he faced dangers from rivers
    - This speaks of natural barriers such as swollen rivers

that he would have encountered in his travels
- Second, he faced dangers from robbers
  - Ancient travelers were often times targets of robbers much like we saw communicated in the Parable of the Good Samaritan
- Third, he faced dangers from his countrymen
  - This points to opposition from the Jews
- Fourth, he faced dangers from the Gentiles
  - Paul's opposition was not only Jewish, it was also Gentile
- Fifth, he faced dangers in the city
  - He faced dangers in the cities he visited much like we read about in Ephesus with the start of a riot
- Sixth, he faced dangers in the wilderness
  - These were dangers he faced in less inhabited regions
- Seventh, he faced dangers on the sea
- Eighth, he faced dangers from false brothers
  - The implication is that there were people within the church who claimed to be brothers in Christ, but actually were not
  - More surprisingly, there were people in the church who posed a real threat to Paul
  - Paul had to deal with threats and danger outside of the church, but also within the church itself
  - This may even allude to the Judaizers in places like Corinth and Galatia

11:27

- Paul now points to some of the other physical hardships that he has encountered
- He mentions having to deal with sleepless nights
- The sleepless nights probably came as a result of his commitment to "more labors"
- He adds that he has also endured "hunger, thirst and going without food"

- Also, he has dealt with exposure
- This speaks of going without clothes as a result of poverty

11:28

- The phrase "apart from such external things" simply means "other things" that he has had to deal with on top of the physical suffering he faced
- The word "pressure" is the idea of feeling a sense of responsibility for something
- Paul felt the weight of his care for the well-being of the church
- The word "concern" is a word that means "worry" or "anxiety"
- Certainly, some of the pressure was his concern for the church at Corinth
- However, there were many other churches that Paul was concerned about
- He had a concern for how the church would receive his teaching and correction
- He had a concern for rivals within the church undermining apostolic authority
- He had a concern for false brethren within those churches
- He had a concern for wolves in sheep's clothing
- He had a concern for the church growing and reaching maturity
- He had a concern for the church and their leadership
- He had a concern for false teaching and false doctrine within the church
- He had a concern for sin within the church
- He had a concern for spiritual attacks from Satan against the church
- He had a concern for sin within the camp
- He had a concern for the persecution of the church
- He had a concern for worldliness invading the church
- He had a concern for unity within the church
- This concern was not just a secondary concern, it was a real pressure that took an emotional toll on him
- Leadership includes bearing the pressure of concern for those you lead and care about

- We see this attitude in Paul's communication with the elder in the church at Ephesus (Acts 20)

11:29

- Here we find two examples of the type of pressure and concern that Paul feels regarding the churches
- First, he said he had concern for those who are weak
- Throughout the Corinthians letters, weakness was something to be embraced because God tends to use the weak things of the world to shame the wise
- Paul had just given a list of his sufferings which would be defined by the world as points of weakness
- Paul felt his own weakness as he underwent those hardships which he listed
- As a result, there may be other Christians who are weak because they are facing trials, hardships or difficulties of their own
- In addition, perhaps the idea of weak here speaks of those who are spiritually weak or immature
- Paul told the Corinthians that to those were weak he became weak
  - **1 Corinthians 9:22 -** ²² To the weak I became weak, that I might win the weak; I have become all things to all men, so that I may by all means save some.
- By contrast, the Judaizers were harsh with those who were weak
- He is saying that he shares with the weak in their weakness
- Secondly, Paul had concern for those led into sin
- The concern is for believers who stumble into sin
- Being led into sin speaks of stumbling in a way that one falls
- Being led into sin indicates that someone else or something else might be the cause of their stumbling
- More specifically, Paul is citing his concern that these Judaizers would lead people in the church away from Jesus
- Paul is not just bothered by this prospect, but he says he has "intense concern"
- The word "intense concern" is the idea of "burning"

11:30

- Now, Paul says that if he is really going to boast he is going to boast in his weakness
- It seems like a contradiction to boast about weakness
- His weakness is what highlights his dependence upon God
- Of course, what he spoke of as weakness, God would define as real strength
- This also shows the difference between Paul and the "super apostles"
- Paul's boasting was in things that the world classified as weak
- Their boasting was on things that elevated themselves

11:31

- This is Paul calling upon God as his witness
- We do not know why Paul feels a need to call upon God's name here to prove he is not lying
- He is not making outrageous claims that elevate him, he is

making claims rooted in weakness

- Perhaps the oath is more connected to what follows

(i.e. heavenly visions and Damascus incident)

11:32-33

- Earlier he had listed several

hardships

- Now, he is going to re-tell some

significant stories

- This is Paul's account of his escape

from Damascus

- Perhaps this is an example of

"dangers in the city"

- In Acts, Luke gives some of the

details of this same event

    - **Acts 9:23-25** - [23] When many days had elapsed, the Jews plotted together to do away with him, [24] but their plot became known to Saul. They were also watching the gates day and night so that they might put him to death; [25] but his disciples took him by night and let him down through *an opening in* the wall, lowering him in a large basket.

- Acts tells us that Paul had confounded the Jews in Damascus through his preaching
- As a result of this, they had planned on killing Paul
- In order to accomplish this plan they enlisted the ethnarch who ordered him to be seized
- The word the NASB translates as "ethnarch" is like a governor or even possibly the ruler of a particular ethnic group within a city
- In the year 66 BC the Roman general Pompey conquered the city of Damascus
- During this first century, the Romans would have allowed King

Aretas to appoint a governor over the city

- The king who is mentioned would be Aretas IV who reigned over the Nabateans (Arabia) from 9 BC to 40 AD
- This means that Paul's escape from Damascus was a couple of years before that 40 AD date
- King Aretas IV's daughter was the wife of Herod Antipas who was Governor of Galilee
- Remember, Herod Antipas divorces her to marry his half-brother's wife (who was also hie niece)[4]
  - **Matthew 14:1-4** - At that time Herod the tetrarch heard the news about Jesus, [2] and said to his servants, "This is John the Baptist; he has risen from the dead, and that is why miraculous powers are at work in him." [3] For when Herod had John arrested, he bound him and put him in prison because of Herodias, the wife of his brother Philip. [4] For John had been saying to him, "It is not lawful for you to have her."
- Paul recounts how some Christian friends hid Paul and then let him down out of a window in a basket so he could escape
- Ancient cities commonly were surrounded by walls and had homes built right on the inside of the wall
- This New Testament story somewhat reminds us of Rahab and the spies (**Joshua 2:15**)

- Some have assumed that

King Aretas may have become
involved in this plot because he

would have some familiarity
with Paul from his time
in Arabia (Galatians 1:17-18).

• Perhaps, Paul left Arabia for

Damascus only to find

Kisan Gate. This is the traditional
site of his escape. It shows a wall in
Damascus like which Paul would
have been let down through.

Opposition from the

Jews and the Governor

• The point once again is

that while Paul has faced
near-death, he has also
had many great
escapes from death

2 Corinthians 12

12:1

- In chapter 11, Paul had already introduced some of his boasting in order to silence his critics
- In chapter 11, the focus was on his sufferings for the cause of the Gospel
- In chapter 12, he will first introduce the idea of his heavenly vision
- On multiple occasions, Paul has made clear that he does not really want to engage in boasting
- He saw that boasting was not profitable for him
- Previously, Paul had spoken of boasting as "foolishness"
- To spend time boasting of one's own accomplishments distracts people from giving glory to God
- Boasting also would run the risk of causing people to follow a man more than they followed Christ
- The only reason that Paul chose to boast was because much more would be lost if he did not defend himself
- Here, he introduces the idea of visions and revelations
- Perhaps, the critics in Corinth had made special claims to some type of supernatural visions themselves in order to strengthen their credibility in the church
- We know from 1 Corinthians that the church did have a special interest in spiritual gifts (1 Corinthians 12-14)
- It was through visions and revelations that God has communicated His truth to the apostles and prophets
    - **Hebrews 1:1** - God, after He spoke long ago to the fathers in the prophets in many portions and in many ways
- Notice the use of the plural for visions and revelations
- It is probable that Paul could claim multiple visions and multiple revelations
- Here, he is going to focus on one such instance
- Paul says that he "received" from the Lord the instructions for the Lord's Supper
    - **1 Corinthians 11:23** - 23 For I received from the Lord that which I also delivered to you, that the Lord Jesus, on the night when He was betrayed, took bread

- Paul says he "received" from the Lord by way of revelation the message and meaning of the Gospel
  - **Galatians 1:11-12** - [11] For I would have you know, brothers *and sisters*, that the gospel which was preached by me is not [l]of human invention. [12] For I neither received it from man, nor was I taught it, but *I received it* through a revelation of Jesus Christ.
  - **1 Corinthians 15:1** - Now I make known to you, brothers *and sisters*, the gospel which I preached to you, which you also received, in which you also stand
- We know of some of the other "revelations" Paul received from God
  - **Galatians 2:2** - [2] It was because of a revelation that I went up; and I submitted to them the gospel which I preach among the Gentiles, but *I did so* in private to those who were of reputation, for fear that somehow I might be running, or had run, in vain.
  - **Acts 9:12** - [12] and he has seen [l]in a vision a man named Ananias come in and lay his hands on him, so that he might regain his sight."
  - **Acts 16:9-10** - [9] And a vision appeared to Paul in the night: a man of Macedonia was standing and pleading with him, and saying, "Come over to Macedonia and help us." [10] When he had seen the vision, we immediately sought to leave for Macedonia, concluding that God had called us to preach the gospel to them.
  - **Acts 18:9-10** - [9] And the Lord said to Paul by a vision at night, "Do not be afraid *any longer*, but go on speaking and do not be silent; [10] for I am with you, and no one will attack you to harm you, for I have many people in this city."
  - **Acts 22:17-21** - [17] "It happened when I returned to Jerusalem and was praying in the temple, that I fell into a trance, [18] and I saw Him saying to me, 'Hurry and get out of Jerusalem quickly, because they will

not accept your testimony about Me.'[19] And I said, 'Lord, they themselves understand that in one synagogue after another I used to imprison and beat those who believed in You. [20] And when the blood of Your witness Stephen was being shed, I also was standing nearby and approving, and watching over the cloaks of those who were killing him.' [21] And He said to me, 'Go! For I will send you far away to the Gentiles.'"

- Acts 26:19 - [19] "For that reason, King Agrippa, I did not prove disobedient to the heavenly vision

- The difference between a vision and a revelation is slight
- The word "vision" is the Greek word *optasia* (ὀπτασία) and it speaks of God causing an image to be clearly displayed in a person's imagination
- The word "revelation" is the Greek word *apokalusis* (ἀποκάλυψις) speaks of new, divine information being made known to a person's understanding
- I would contend that new "revelation" from God is something that was unique to an apostle
- Therefore, perhaps some of Paul's critics could claim to have had some type of vision, they did not receive new revelation from God

12:2

- Some people may assume that when Paul tells of this event in the third person that he is speaking of an event involving someone else
- However, I believe when Paul says, "I know a man" we believe that the man he is speaking of is himself
- Paul says that this heavenly vision occurred fourteen years prior to writing 2 Corinthians
- We dated the writing of 2 Corinthians at 57 AD. Therefore, 14 years prior would have put this heavenly vision taking place in the year 43 AD.
- It seems that Paul's re-telling of this particular vision makes

clear that these types of experiences are not common
- Paul does not give us specific details of what information he received or what exactly he saw
- In fact, Paul is not able to clearly tell his readers whether this was a spiritual, out-of-body experience only or whether he was actually bodily taken up to the third Heaven
- Paul says that he was "caught up"
- The word used is the Greek word *harpazo* which is the same word used to describe Philip being snatched away following the baptism of the Ethiopian Eunuch (Acts 8:39)
- The picture is also of something that happened suddenly
- The Greek indicates that this was something done to him, not something he did himself
- This further highlights that Paul was not boasting in something he accomplished, but something God did
- The Jews commonly used the picture of three Heavens
- The phrase "the third Heaven" speaks of the place where God dwells
- They spoke of the first Heaven being the atmosphere, where the birds fly and where the clouds are
- The second heaven spoke of where the stars and the sun reside

12:3-4

- Once again, Paul repeats his uncertainty about the exact nature of this heavenly vision
- He also repeats the idea of his being "caught up"
- Rather than use the phrase "third heaven", this time he uses the term "paradise"
- The Jewish idea was that paradise was the abode of the righteous dead
- Jesus used the word "paradise" in this way when speaking to the thief on the cross (Luke 23:43)
- Paul's only description of this vision is that he heard "inexpressible words"
- What Paul saw both could not be described and was forbidden to be described

- The idea is most likely that he heard and saw things in his vision that lack adequate words to describe (*rhemata arretos*)
- The issue with the inexpressible words was not his ability to understand what he saw, but in his ability to communicate it fairly
- It also may be true that he was commanded and forbidden to relay the exact nature of his vision
- John was not permitted to share all that he saw either
  - **Revelation 10:4** - [4]When the seven peals of thunder had spoken, I was about to write; and I heard a voice from heaven, saying, "Seal up the things which the seven peals of thunder have spoken, and do not write them."

- Paul was only allowed to reveal to others what he was permitted to speak

12:5

- Paul, who was reluctant to boast says that he will boast of "such a man" who had such an experience
- Of course, the man he is speaking of is himself
- He then says that he will only boast of his weakness
- He will speak some more about his weakness
- Paul will focus on his weaknesses so that God will get the attention and credit

12:6

- Paul will again speak of being reluctant to engage in boasting
- There is such a thing as foolish boasting
- Evidently this was the tactic of some of the Judaizers
- It also seems that Paul is suggesting that they either had lied or exaggerated in order to elevate themselves
- It is telling that Paul has the incredible vision and he only spends four verses talking about it
- Most people would spend a great length of time talking about

this type of experience
- Even in this vision, it is not put forth as an accomplishment of Paul's but something done by God in spite of Paul
- Paul does not want to highlight himself any more than necessary to silence his opponents
- He makes clear that he refrains from going deeper in this boasting so that no person would place him higher than they should

12:7

- Paul now shifts to speaking about what he will call his "thorn in the flesh"
- The purpose of this thorn in the flesh was to keep him from becoming exalted
- Perhaps in wake of all that he had just boasted in, there would be a temptation to start to think that he is really something special
- God gave Paul this thorn to keep him humble
- Sometimes suffering comes into our lives because we live in a fallen world
- Sometimes suffering comes into the world because of our sin or the sin of someone else
- Sometimes suffering comes into our lives to strengthen our character
- For Paul, suffering came to keep him humble and so that God would get the glory through him
- Paul describes the thorn as "a messenger from Satan to torment him"
- The word "torment" is the Greek word *kolaphizo* (κολαφίζω) which means "to strike with the fist
- Paul saw that this thorn was some attack that came from Satan
- This reminds us somewhat of the attack from Satan brought against Job
- We do not know exactly what this thorn in the flesh was
- The word "thorn" (*skolops*) is only used here and has the meaning of "a pointed object"
- Many people have speculated what this might be pointing to in

Paul's life
- The idea that the thorn was "in the flesh" gives us the idea that this was something that physically affected Paul
- Some people have interpreted the thorn to point to persecutions or opposition that Paul faced
- Some people have interpreted this to be some type of sickness of physical problem
- Descriptions of these physical problems have ranged from an eye problem, to a speech impediment, to a disease like malaria or epilepsy
- Some have speculated that it was this physical malady that brought him to Galatia to which he referred to in the book of Galatians
    - **Galatians 4:12-15** - ¹² I beg of you, brothers *and sisters*, become as I *am*, for I also *have become* as you *are*. You have done me no wrong; ¹³ but you know that it was because of a bodily illness that I preached the gospel to you the first time; ¹⁴ and you did not despise that which was a trial to you in my bodily condition, nor express contempt, but you received me as an angel of God, as Christ Jesus *Himself*. ¹⁵ Where then is that sense of blessing you had? For I testify about you that, if possible, you would have torn out your eyes and given them to me.
- The above passage may also imply that the problem was an eyesight problem
- Paul's mention of writing in large letters also hints at an eyesight issue
    - **Galatians 6:11** - See with what large letters I have written to you with my own hand!
- Early traditions such as the one espoused by Tertullian were that the issue was earaches or headaches[5]
- Any attempt to nail this down would be mere conjecture
- There are many possible answers, and had it been important to know the exact idea, Paul would have communicated it
- We reject the idea that this was a sinful struggle that Paul dealt with because, it is out of God's nature to be okay leaving such a

struggle

- It seems that whatever this thorn was, it was a constant aggravation to Paul

12:8

- While we do not know what the thorn was, we do not that on three occasions, Paul pleaded with God to remove it
- We do not know why this prayer was limited to three different occasions rather than a daily petition
- Perhaps this shows that this was some issue that flared up on occasion
- Paul probably prayed for the removal of the thorn because he believed it hindered his ministry
- Perhaps it was that Paul had resigned himself to the fact that this thorn had a purpose

12:9

- The answer to Paul's pleading for the removal of this thorn was "no"
- Jesus prayed in the garden for "this cup to pass from me" but God said "no"
- Moses was told "no" to entering the Promised Land
- God does not always say "yes" to our requests
- The thorn was serving a useful purpose in Paul's life
- Specifically, Paul was told "my grace is sufficient for you, for power is perfected in weakness"
- God has always been willing to use weakness
- Philip Hughes says of this response to Paul: "this is the summit of the epistle, the lofty peak from which the whole is viewed in true proportion. From this vantage-point the entire range of Paul's apostleship is seen in focus – His calling, his conversion, his weakness, his trials, his labors, his conquests and his exaltations – all fall into place; and as the splendor of the sun lights up and transfigures the dark ravines of a great mountain, so the grace of God transfuses and triumphs over, and even

through, what is least impressive in the apostle's constitution."
- The thorn highlighted Paul's weakness so that God's power might be on greater display
- Paul's weaknesses made it clear who was working in and through his life
- Although Paul may have seen this thorn as a hindrance to his ministry, God is making clear that it is actually a help
- The grace spoken of here is God's sustaining grace
- God does not always deliver from something, but often will sustain us through it
- The idea is also that although God did not give Paul what he asked for, He was giving him the strength to endure the thorn in the flesh
- The thorn was used to keep Paul humble and God always uses the humble
- It is through Paul's boasting of his own weaknesses that God's power and greatness is on display
- We may experience similar trials or physical limitations that we perceive as hindrances or annoyances, but God can use them to display His greatness
- Paul's is not a case of one who became bitter through suffering, but rather of one who kept serving through his trials

12:10

- It is for the reason of God's power being on display that Paul has learned to be content with his own weaknesses
- His weakness includes the thorn in the flesh
- He speaks of some of the things that he endures so that God may get greater attention
- He refers to five things he endured for the sake of Christ
    - Weaknesses
    - Insults
    - Distresses
    - Persecutions
    - Difficulties
- All of those things may be enough to cause most people to feel

defeated or to stop doing what they are doing
- He is content because he is doing what he can for Christ's sake
- We can endure a whole lot more when we know we are doing so for the sake of Christ versus
- So many people struggle to endure life's difficulties because they cannot view them through the perspective of "for Christ's sake"
- He can be content with weakness because his aim is not himself being built up, but rather God being lifted up

12:11

- Paul once again admits to being foolish by engaging in this boasting
- This is the sixth time in the section on boasting that Paul used the word "foolish" to describe is (11:1, 11:16a, 11:16b, 11:19, 12:6, 12:11)
- When he introduced this idea in 11:1, Paul asked the church bear with him in "a little foolishness"
- As Paul sums up what he has written in the last section, he seems to be uncomfortable with the boasting that he engaged in
- He goes further and say that it is their actions that forced his hand and made him have to boast
- In fact, the word for compelled is *anagkazo* (ἀναγκάζω) which means to force, to compel or to drive
- Paul points some of the blame at the church at Corinth for this whole section
- They made it necessary for him to boast because they did not defend him
- They had bought into the boasting by these super apostles and probably also had their view of Paul affected
- Paul says that they should have commended him
- Perhaps Paul had in mind the wisdom that Solomon spoke of
    - **Proverbs 27:2** - Let another praise you, and not your own mouth; A stranger, and not your own lips.
- They should have stood up for him in the face of these opponents

- They should have been able to testify to these Judaizers the things Paul boasted about in his letter
- They could have listed all of these things that Paul boasted about and more
- As we saw earlier, the idea of commending was supposed to be something that someone else did on your behalf
- He also addresses the issue of his comparison to these super apostles
- He claims that he is not inferior to the super apostles in any way
- In any way that you might measure the two, Paul is not inferior
- Here lies the difference between Paul and these people. Paul does not claim to be superior to these super apostles, but he does insist that he is not inferior
- There is a big difference in their approach
- The super apostles had built themselves up by tearing Paul down and claiming superiority
- Paul does not need superiority although on his own merits and based on where God had placed him, he may have had a case for it
- Paul says that he is not inferior even though he is nothing
- Paul certainly did not have an inflated view of himself
- Other places he spoke of his weakness and nothingness before God
    - **1 Corinthians 15:9** - [9] For I am the least of the apostles, and not fit to be called an apostle, because I persecuted the church of God.
    - **2 Corinthians 3:5** - [5] Not that we are adequate in ourselves to consider anything as *coming* from ourselves, but our adequacy is from God
- If he being nothing is not inferior to the super apostles, he is implying that at best they are nothings too
- As it relates to his apostleship, Paul is willing to defend
- He understood that all he was came from God

12:12

- This is one of the major reasons the Corinthians should have

- been able to defend Paul to these super apostles
- Paul claims that he performed the signs of a true apostle during the 18 months that he was among them
- If there are signs of a true apostle, this must mean that there is a way to distinguish true apostles from false apostles
- Paul is plainly making the claim that he is a true apostle and furthermore that the church knows it very well
- The signs of a true apostle speaks specifically of apostolic miracles
- One of the distinct traits of an apostle was that the spiritually gifts could be passed on by the laying on of their hands
    - **Acts 8:18** - [18] Now when Simon saw that the Spirit was bestowed through the laying on of the apostles' hands, he offered them money
- These miracles were evidence that Paul was what he claimed to be
- Non-apostles were able to perform miracles too
- Some people could perform false miracles
    - **2 Thessalonians 2:9** - [9] *that is,* the one whose coming is in accord with the activity of Satan, with all power and signs and false wonders
- The question here is not just discerning between a true apostle and a false apostle, but also discerning between true miracles and false miracles
- Perhaps it was not just the miracles by themselves, but the miracles combined with his character, his claims, his suffering, and all these other things that validated him as an apostle
- Paul even says that these miracles were performed with "all perseverance"
- This indicates that they were done over an extended period of time and in the midst of trials, difficulty, persecution and opposition
- In fact, the purpose of miracles is to strengthen the evidence of new revelation
- The Corinthians themselves had been eyewitnesses to proofs of Paul's apostolic authority
- Paul had made similar statements to other churches

- - - ○ **Romans 15:18-19** - [18] For I will not presume to speak of anything except what Christ has accomplished through me, resulting in the obedience of the Gentiles by word and deed, [19] in the power of signs and wonders, in the power of the Spirit; so that from Jerusalem and round about as far as Illyricum I have fully preached the gospel of Christ.
    - ○ **1 Thessalonians 1:5** - [5] for our gospel did not come to you in word only, but also in power and in the Holy Spirit and with full conviction; just as you know what kind of men we proved to be among you for your sake.
- He defines the signs of a true apostle by three different terms
- These three terms all describe the miracle itself
- They are different angles of the same thing
- The miracles is the event itself or a mighty act which points to God's power
- The wonder is the reaction to the miracles. It refers to the awe that the miracles produces
- The sign is the purpose of the miracle
- The sign points to the things
- We do not know what miracles were performed in Corinth, but Paul is claiming that he gave them ample evidence when he was among them
- Remember, the purpose of a miracles was to spark belief and confirm coming, new revelation from God or a messenger from God

12:13

- Perhaps one the criticisms that the "super apostles" brought against Paul to the church was that he treated the church there differently than he treated other churches
- Perhaps they felt that Paul had slighted them in some way
- Paul states very clearly that he did not treat them or consider them to be inferior to other churches
- When Paul speaks of "becoming a burden" he is speaking of

- working as a tentmaker and not taking pay from the church
- Specifically, one of the issues that Paul has had to deal with was the issue of working a job to supplement his income
- The reason he did this was not to insult them, but rather to not burden them
- There is no chance that the church actually saw this as a wrong done by Paul
- There is also no chance that Paul in any way thinks he did something wrong
- He posed the same idea earlier
    - **2 Corinthians 11:7** - [7] Or did I commit a sin in humbling myself so that you might be exalted, because I preached the gospel of God to you without charge?
- So, when he asks that they "forgive him this wrong" I do not believe that he is conceding that he did something wrong to them
- The phrase here is filled with sarcasm
- He did not really need to apologize for acting selflessly and sacrificially
- If anyone has need of asking forgiveness, it is the Corinthians who need to ask Paul for forgiveness

12:14

- Here, we have introduced the idea of another visit that Paul wanted to make to the church at Corinth
- Paul says that this would be his third visit to them
- The first visit was his initial visit where he established the church and spent 18 months. This is recorded in Acts 18:1-17
- The second visit was an unplanned and painful visit in between the writing of 1 Corinthians and 2 Corinthians
- As he prepares them for this visit, he once again feels it is necessary to spend time defending his practice of not taking pay from them
- He declares to them very clearly that he plans on maintaining this same practice when he comes again

- Notice that Paul describes more of his reasoning
- He says that "I do not seek what is yours, but you"
- The thing that is "yours" is their money
- His desire is not a paycheck, but rather brotherhood
- They may have perceived Paul's not taking pay from the church as a slight upon themselves, but Paul says that it is just the opposite
- Paul could never be accused of being greedy or money hungry
- Now, taking a paycheck from the church would not have been contradictory to this desire either
- Just because one is paid does not mean that they do it because they desire someone's money more than they desire the person
- John Chryostom paraphrases Paul's statement here: "I seek greater things; souls instead of goods; instead of gold, salvation."
- Perhaps the statement "I do not seek what is yours, but you…" is a contrast between himself and the "super apostles" who wanted what is theirs more than the people themselves
- To make the intent of his decision even more clear he presents them with an argument
- The argument uses the illustration of a parent-child relationship
- He points to the idea of inheritance. Parents are not the heirs of their children. Children are the heirs of their parents
- He is saying that "parents give to and provide for and save up for their children. Children are not expected to provide for their parents"
- Paul is the spiritual parent who sees it as his function to protect and take care of his spiritual children

12:15

- Here, Paul still sounds very much like a parent speaking to his child
- As their spiritual father, Paul says that he is willing to spend everything for the Corinthians
- He was not just willing to not take from them; he was willing to give them everything he has and everything he earns

- He even took it a step further and says he is willing to "expend myself as well"
- The idea is that he is willing to go as far as give his life for the Corinthians
- This does not just point to a willingness to die, but also a willingness to "exhaust" himself for them or wear himself out for them
- Paul's commitment to the church and his affection for them is so strong, it would stop at nothing to demonstrate love
- He is willing to do this "most gladly"
- He is not just willing to reluctantly spend and be expended, but he is willing to do so happily
- I wonder if the critics, those super apostles could say this
- At the end of this verse, he poses an ironic question
- He asks them if his great love for them will cause them to love him less?
- One would think that such a great display of affection and sacrificial love would be returned with great levels of love

12:16

- The phrase "be that as it may" speaks of their decreasing love in wake of his increasing love
- Once again he makes clear that he was never a burden upon the church
- When we read the phrase "crafty fellow that I am, I took you in by deceit" should be read as a quotation coming from the "super apostles"
- They had spread the lie in the church at Corinth that Paul's motives were insincere and that he had endeared them to himself through "deceit"
- The word "crafty" is not the idea of being wise, but being treacherous and sneaky
- The word "deceit" is a hunting term which carries the idea of setting a trap to catch prey
- Specifically in mind was the collection for the poor saints in Jerusalem

- The accusation was that this collection was all a set-up by Paul
  to make some type of profit and that his behavior among them
  was all a part of this elaborate scheme to squander money from
  the church
- This idea is clearly false and Paul has proven it false in every
  possible way

12:17

- It is possible that the accusation made against Paul was that he
  exploited the church through some of the people he had sent to
  them
- The answer to his question of whether he exploited them was
  clearly a "no"
- He is calling upon the church to produce evidence of this
  exploitation

12:18

- Now, he goes from vague to specific
- He specifically is asking if the church is willing to suggest that
  Titus was a part of a scheme to defraud the church
- Once again, their answer was "no"
- They would not have been willing to speak beyond generalities
  in their accusations against Paul because their accusations were
  untrue
- The church at Corinth knew Titus and his character first hand
- From what we can gather about their interaction with Titus, the
  church at Corinth had a positive relationship with him
    - **2 Corinthians 7:6-7** - But God, who comforts
      the [b]depressed, comforted us by the coming
      of Titus; [7] and not only by his coming, but also by
      the comfort with which he was comforted in you, as
      he reported to us your longing, your mourning, your
      zeal for me; so that I rejoiced even more.
    - **2 Corinthians 7:13** - For this reason we have
      been comforted. And besides our comfort, we

rejoiced even much more for the joy of Titus,
because his spirit has been refreshed by you all

- Paul asks one more rhetorical question here
- He asks, "did we not act in the same spirit and walk in the same steps?"
- The question assumed a "yes" answer here
- He is saying that Titus in him shared the same goals, showed the same godly attitude and had similar character

12:19

- The question here is somewhat surprising
- He states, "all this time you have been thinking that we are defending ourselves to you"
- At first glance the apparent answer would be "yes"
- It seemed as though he has been defending himself since chapter 10
- However, Paul's point is that he really does not have to defend himself to them
- The Corinthians are not who is accountable to
- It is God that he must answer to for his conduct
- This is what he means when he said "it is in the sight of God we have been speaking"
- He is telling them that he is not trying to be defensive in that the charges against him are not one bit credible
- He is writing due to his concern for them, not out of a concern for his own reputation
- The defense of himself was not for himself, but it was for the strengthening of the church at Corinth
- It was harmful to the church at Corinth to follow these critics and distance themselves from Paul

12:20

- Now, Paul speaks of what his concern is when he arrives in Corinth for his visit
- The phrase "for I am afraid" gives off the idea that it is well

- within the realm of possibility
- He first says that he is afraid to find the church "not as I wish"
- In other words, he is suggesting that it is possible that the church still had not straightened out many of their internal problems
- To go along with that, he says that they might as a result "find Paul not as they wish"
- This seems to imply that they may wish to have a happy, cordial visit with Paul, but if things are a mess in the church, they will not encounter Paul in the way that they wish they could
- Paul holds out the possibility that his coming would be as a stern disciplinarian
- He mentions eight of the possible things he is concerned about finding in the church
- This is not intended to be an exhaustive list of what he might find, but it does convey some of the issue at hand
- First, he speaks of strife
- Strife implies that they were not getting along
- Second, he speaks of jealousy
- This is that they wanted what someone else has
- Perhaps it was jealousy over spiritual gifts or something of the sort
- Third, he speaks of angry tempers
- Fourth, he speaks of disputes
- Fifth, he speaks of slanders
- Sixth, he speaks of gossip
- Seventh, he speaks of arrogance
- Eighth, he speaks of disturbances
- All of these point to some type of threat to internal, interpersonal harmony in the church
- These types of conditions may already be present in the church
- Paul is hoping that much of this is straightened out before he arrives

12:21

- Evidently the problems are not just interpersonal threats to the church's unity

- There is also ongoing, outright immorality in the church
- Paul speaks of being afraid that he will have to come and deal with those sins as well
- He is concerned that finding the church in this way would be humiliating for him
- It could be humiliating because he had spoken so well of the church to other people
- It could be humiliating because of the mourning that would come with the response
- It could be humiliating because of the impact it would have on the church's reputation
- It could be humiliating because he expects better fruit from his labors
- Notice however that the humiliation is not done by the Corinthians, but by God
- Perhaps the idea is more that as God disciplines the unrepentant or "gives them over" it would produce great grief for Paul
- The correction of the sin would come with real mourning over it
- The mourning here is a godly sorrow over unrepented sin
- It is fine to correct and rebuke sin, but perhaps it should be accompanied by mourning as well
- The mourning isn't just over sin, it is over unrepented sin
- He mentions three specific classes of sins which have been a part of the church's past, which he fears are still a part of the church's present
- First, he mentions impurity (*akatharsia*)
- This speaks of any type of sexual impurity
- Second, he mentions immorality (*porneia*)
- This is not just general immoral behavior, but specifically sexually immoral behavior
- Third, he mentions sensuality (*aselgeia*)
- This is licentiousness which speaks of behavior that is shocking to public decency
- All three of these are sins of a sexual nature
- These same three sins begin Paul's list of sins of the flesh in Galatians 5
    - **Galatians 5:19** - [19] Now the deeds of the flesh are

evident, which are: immorality, impurity, sensuality

- We know that the church had issues with sexual immorality in the past
- In 1 Corinthians 5, Paul had to write to address a specific sexual sin
- In 1 Corinthians 6, Paul said, "that's what some of you were" when speaking of immorality
- Perhaps there were other issues taking place in the church
- Perhaps some of the issues were connected with the false teachers in the church

2 Corinthians 13

13:1

- Paul is continuing to give some warnings to the church to prepare for his visit
- Paul certainly is giving a very strong warning, but based off of the earlier report he received from Titus, we might expect a positive result
- In other words, it is likely that the church was in the process of getting their act together even as Paul wrote these words
- This is a reminder for them to keep straightening out their issues
- The language here is almost like that of a person taking someone to court
- In verse 1, Paul also quotes from Deuteronomy 19:15
- The idea of the Old Testament reference was that it would be better for a guilty person to be unpunished than an innocent person to be convicted based off of a slanderous accusation
- Paul is making the point that the issues that he has are not unfounded issues based on hearsay
- Perhaps the idea of the three witnesses even is pointing to his three visits to Corinth
- Paul's point seems to be that their own private dispute will be

dealt with publicly when he arrives

- Furthermore, Paul can call witnesses against them
- He has witnesses such as Titus and Timothy
- This is quite the contrast from the baseless accusations that the "super apostles" in Corinth were making against Paul

13:2

- Here, we get some clue about the nature of Paul's intermediate visit to Corinth
- He obviously had presented them with some stern warnings
- He tells the church that he is issuing this warning in advance of his third visit to them
- The warning had to do with the church dealing with sin within the church
- He speaks of "those who have sinned in the past"
- This is not just a call to some type of punitive punishment
- It is a call to deal with sin that took place in the past, but remained unrepented of
- We do not know what he has in mind
- Perhaps it goes back to the immoral brother in 1 Corinthians 5
- Perhaps the issues are more in general in regard to unrepented and continuous sin
- Not only was it a call for the church to deal with its own issues, but it was a warning that if they did not, he would exert his authority as an apostle
- Notice the warning was not just to the ones guilty of the unrepented sin, it was a warning to the "rest as well"
- These are people in the church who are guilty by way of their toleration and indifference
- By saying "I will not spare anyone" he is making it very clear that church discipline or even excommunication may be necessary
- We even have two examples in the New Testament of a physical punishment or act of judgment
    - Ananias and Sapphira - Acts 5:1-11
    - Elymas - Acts 13:6-12

- If this letter did not do the final trick of brining about repentance, Paul would deal with it in person during his third visit
- Make no mistake, Paul does not desire this type of confrontation. He desires repentance.

13:3

- Paul's critics in Corinth had sown seeds of doubt regarding his apostleship and authority
- Despite showing "signs of a true apostle" among them (12:12), they wanted further proof that he had this type of authority
- They wanted to see that he had the authority to correct and discipline them
- Furthermore, they wanted proof that he spoke with Christ's authority
- They are suggesting that Paul may be an un-inspired teacher
- Perhaps it was Paul's patience, gentleness and meekness in dealing with the church up to this point that caused more doubts to arise about Paul's authority or whether Christ was speaking through him
- Although the church may have pointed to Paul's weakness, he points out that Christ is not weak at all
- Christ had shown Himself mighty in their midst not only through Paul, but also through the spiritual gifts that they had been given by an apostle

13:4

- The only defense Paul will make here of this is a parallel between Christ and himself
- The point is that the Corinthians and Paul differ greatly in their understanding of power and their view of weakness
- The Corinthians saw power as dominance
- Paul sees power as being perfected through man's weakness
- Paul said that Jesus himself was crucified because of weakness
- Now, we know that Jesus was not weak or helpless, but He

willingly went to the cross
- Jesus was not actually weak, but He did make the choice to allow Himself to be crucified
- The phrase "He lives because" points to His resurrection and His reign as Lord of lords
- Perhaps any onlooker on the day of Jesus' crucifixion may have seen weakness, but the resurrection showed His real power
- He had power to lay down his life and power to take it up again
- Notice Paul's connection to himself, "for we also"
- Paul says that "we are weak in Him"
- Paul knew that his own weakness was a means of displaying God's power
- The display of God's power speaks to the resurrection
- Paul is not claiming to personally have power, but that the power of God is at work through weakness
- Paul has been following Christ's example. The Corinthians perceive it to be weakness, just like many might see Jesus' death as an example of weakness

13:5

- Paul completely flips the script on the Corinthians
- In verse 3, Paul speaks about the fact that they want proof that Christ is in Him and speaking through him
- Now, Paul says, they should be able to prove that Christ is in them as well
- They should be focused on themselves, not Paul
- Paul calls upon the Christians in Corinth to test themselves
- Paul told the Galatians to test their own work
  - **Galatians 6:4** - But each one must examine his own work, and then he will have *reason for* boasting in regard to himself alone, and not in regard to another.
- The test is to determine if they are in the faith
- The idea is to test whether they are really saved
- It seems evident that a person could call themselves a Christian, attend the local church and not really be in the faith
- Paul does not provide them with the appropriate test questions or

some type of checklist
- The way that they could test this would be by the fruits being produced in their own lives
- He not only calls upon them to test themselves, but then he commands them to examine themselves as well
- The examination is a heart inventory
- This is something that an outsider is not able to do, it has to be a personal inventory
- Paul does not seem to expect them to actually fail this type of test
- His point is that Christ is in them and this should be evident by their conduct

13:6

- Now, Paul goes back to their charge against him
- He says that he wants them to know that in an equivalent test, he does not fail it either
- His test is not about being in the faith though, it is about being an apostle and speaking the words of Christ
- Another difference between the tests is that the Corinthians were to test themselves. The Corinthians were also doing the test regarding Paul's apostleship. Paul was not testing himself
- Don't miss the context here. Paul's test and the Corinthian's personal test are connected
- If they pass the test to see that Christ is in them, it in turn must mean that Paul passes their test as well
- If they all claim to pass their test to see that they are in the faith, that cannot possibly mean Paul is a sham apostle or else they would all fail the test

13:7

- This verse is a bit more difficult to understand
- Paul begins by telling the Corinthians that he hopes that in response to this letter that they do no wrong
- The "no wrong" speaks of them stopping doing whatever evil

practices were taking place among them
- If they do what is right, that would obviously change the tone and nature of his visit
- The only negative that the tenor of the visit changing is that it would cause Paul to miss the chance to prove to the Corinthians that he indeed can be very bold when face to face
- If they repent, and if they do what is right, Paul will still not have proof to some that he is not weak in person
- His main point is that his greater concern is that the Corinthians be approved by God due to their character than he be approved by them as a legitimate apostle
- Paul's focus is never on making himself look good

13:8

- Paul's end goal is the truth
- Here, it speaks of the truth of the Gospel
- Paul does have authority, but his authority is beholden to the truth
- Any real apostle is going to speak the truth
- True apostles are more focused on the truth than they are upon themselves

13:9

- Once again Paul speaks of how it is in his own weakness that Christ's power is on display in a greater way
- This may be Paul's explanation of why he would be happy to not be severe with them in person
- The goal of this letter was to bring repentance
- He then says that his goal is that they be made "complete"
- The word here is the Greek word *katartizo* which has the idea of restoring walls, preparing a remedy, mending nets or resetting a dislocated bone. It is the idea of restoring something that is damaged
- Paul is suggesting that something has not been right, but that he is hoping that things will be mended

13:10

- Remember, the criticism of Paul was about his weakness in person and his boldness in writing
- He explains that he writes boldly so that he does not have to be severe when he is there
- Paul would love to come to them gently
- He further states that any use of severity would be consistent with authority that God had specifically given to him as an apostle
- Paul would not be usurping authority in discipling the church in some way
- The purpose of the use of the authority was for building up the church not tearing it down
- Even though the severity may include discipline or removal of some for the church, it is all for building up the church
- This is a great picture of the use of Biblical authority
- Biblical authority may include discipline or correction, but its goal must be for building up

13:11

- Paul gives five final charges to the church
- First, he tells them to rejoice
- This is a present imperative which means the command is to "continue rejoicing"
- The presence of real joy is a major key to real blessing from God
- Second, he instructs that they be made complete
- In verse 9, the idea of being complete was mentioned as well
- It is speaking of mending or restoring things
- The instruction is to "keep mending things in the church"
- Third, he tells them to be comforted
- They may need comfort in the midst of the pains that come from mending things
- They may need comforted so that their sorrow over sin does not carry them to the point where they do not trust in God's grace or to be overcome by guilt

- Fourth, he tells them to be like-minded
- One of the major problems going back even to 1 Corinthians was factions in the church
- Here, Paul instructs the church to think the same way as each other
- Fifth, he tells them to live in peace
- He is calling for them to put an end to the internal conflict and be at peace with one another
- He follows these five things with a clear result of what will happen if the heed his advice
- The blessing is that the God of peace and love will be with them all
- Obviously, this blessing is conditional

13:12-14

- These are the final greetings of the letter
- In several other NT letters, the call is made to extend a greeting of a "holy kiss"
- This was a customary eastern greeting
- The kiss was a sign of greeting, love, respect and acceptance
- It is a "holy kiss" in that it was not associated with romance or perversion
- He also passes on regards and love from the saints all over the world where he has been

13:14

- He closes with a special benediction asking for special blessing upon the Corinthians
- Paul asks for blessing even upon people who have challenged him, opposed him and slandered him